GARDENS
of the
ITALIAN LAKES

GARDENS *of the* ITALIAN LAKES

STEVEN DESMOND

PHOTOGRAPHS BY
MARIANNE MAJERUS

FRANCES LINCOLN

CONTENTS

To Roger Oxtoby
my first head gardener
who taught me all I know

INTRODUCTION

There are many lakes in Italy, and it is a country famous around the world for its gardens. Everyone, however, knows what are meant by the gardens of the Italian Lakes. These are the subalpine lakes of Lombardy and Piedmont in the far north, right on the Swiss border, to the north of Milan. Whatever the charms of such lakes as Garda, Orta and many others in the north, equally framed in mountain scenery and overlooked by interesting villas, castles and fishing villages, the lakes of choice for the garden-lover are Como and Maggiore.

Both these great lakes are easily approached from the Lombard plain from the south. Indeed, those travelling up to either lake from the airports of Milan must begin to wonder at first whether they have misread the literature, so pancake-flat is the countryside, and so busy with traffic. This is not the laid-back Italy of the brochures, but the business end of the country. Soon, however, the peaks begin to appear through the haze, and a different world beckons, one in which the speed of travel is dictated by the chug of a boat across a lake. It is this situation among the foothills of the Alps which brings the crowds in the first place. The natives come here in droves in the summer to escape the humid heat of the plain and the city. Nothing could be imagined more different from the broad and earnest streets of Milan. The foreigner is enticed by the magical prospect of sunshine and scenery, with the added attraction of relative ease of access. The public transport network is excellent, and motorways come near enough to make life convenient without those unwelcome concrete stilts intruding on the view.

LEFT The mountains of Lombardy rise behind the island terraces of Isola Bella on Lake Maggiore. The combination of the scenery, the climate and the presence of patrons willing to make extravagant gardens and receive visitors has proved a powerful attraction for centuries.

Once here, half the fun is in travelling about on the public service boats. It is much more civilized than battling through lakeside villages in a hired car. It is a straightforward business on the boats, with their regular timetables, affordable fares and choice of where to sit or stand.

For a grandstand view of the islands, gardens and villas, the boat trip is hard to beat and enables the novice visitor to make more sense of the context of each place, and to see the relationship between one and another. However lovely a particular garden, it gains enormously from its relationship with its setting – on a shore, on a headland or on an island. The scramble for possession of some of these sites in the past was intense.

TOP Lake Como is glimpsed through a haze of azalea (*Rhododendron*) flowers in the garden of the Villa Carlotta, near Cadenabbia, in April. The ever-changing clouds hanging on the distant mountain peaks suggest the perpetual uncertainty of the local climate.

ABOVE Edwardian bourgeois pleasure-seekers glide away from the gardens of the Villa Carlotta on Lake Como in a postcard view from the early twentieth century. The lake steamer was an established and respectable mode of travel on the lakes from the 1830s.

Lago di Como - MENAGGIO

There are down sides to some of these questions for the owners. An island in a lake is an impractical place to live. Everything has to be brought, slowly and awkwardly. Imagine what it was like when statues in the garden on Isola Bella were blown down recently. All the repair materials had to be delivered from the mainland, even though it was only a few hundred metres away. Construction machinery needed to be ferried over, dismantled, carried up the steps, reassembled . . . you have the idea. It is necessary to live with a permanent particular mindset. At no point did the house or garden close to carry out the works. Life must go on, and there are plenty of people who, like me, enjoy watching the craft skills of conservation workers in action.

The climate is of course a vital ingredient here. Many *forestieri* labour under the delusion that the sun always shines in Italy, but this is not the case. These lakes have an unexpected microclimate, one in which winters tend to be dry, and summers wet. The wettest months of the year on both lakes are May and August, just the two you might have

been considering for a visit. And how wet does it get? Very. Lake Maggiore, for example, receives an annual average rainfall of 2.3 metres / 90 inches. That is a lot, considerably more, for example, than the famously wet Lake District in England; and most of it falls during the summer months. Not surprisingly, there are periodic monumental floods and storms, with several examples of both in recent years. So would I still recommend a visit? Absolutely, on the basis of many years' experience. The weather will probably be lovely, but have your waterproofs somewhere near at hand.

One major benefit of all this rain is the singular beauty of the gardens. Visitors from dry countries will find that their eyes hurt from the brightness of the greenery everywhere. Edith Wharton thought there could be no pleasure in seeing an Italian lawn as brown as a doormat, and she was right, but things stay green here for the usual reason. It is a decisive advantage. Despite the towering mountains all around, covered with snow for much of the year, even a superficial examination of the tree shoots shows that frost damage is slight, and that the growing season is long.

A big part of this mildness is the result of the sheer surface area of water, with its moderating effect on the range of temperatures, like the sea. This effect is all the more noticeable on the islands, where the vegetation is perceptibly

---

ABOVE The *Lariana* steams into Menaggio on Lake Como to return its passengers to their lakeside hotels after a day of garden visiting. The rowing boats hired by couples for the same purpose are about to lose some of their dignity in its wake.

more vigorous, despite the thin soil overlying bedrock. The island gardens record fewer frosts each year than those on the mainland. In combination with this balance, the sheer power of the Italian sun, pushing away the morning mists, has a dramatic effect on the vegetation, bringing plants into flower longer and earlier than in more northerly latitudes.

A pleasant place to be, then, on the whole. And in what style are these gardens? Well, Italian gardens are famous around the world for certain things. The foreigner dreaming on his chaise longue thinks of terraces, mosaics, lemon (*Citrus × limon*) trees, fountains, twirly box (*Buxus*) parterres, all looking out over glorious scenery, but perhaps everything not in the best of repair, and a bit short of decorative plant interest. Some of the famous desiderata are here in abundance: between these pages are lots of terraces and parterres, and there is certainly no shortage of spectacular scenery, yet these gardens are different. Alongside the justly famous Italian tradition, the very foundation of European garden history, there is another world here – that of the

plant-lover. Italy is not a nation of garden visitors, but here it has responded magnificently to the demand, and so we see immensely rich collections especially of trees and shrubs organized into handsome layouts, often well labelled and, typically, immaculately maintained. Part of the reason for this is the long-standing influence of foreign owners such as Neil McEacharn of the Villa Táranto, who, unwilling to adapt to native tradition, insisted on laying out Italy's only double herbaceous borders in his garden, and forming a woodland garden around them, as if he were in Britain. But it would be wrong to attribute all of this to the work of outsiders: not far

---

ABOVE Part of the wonder of the garden climate on the lakes is that big clay pots of lemon (*Citrus × limon*) trees can be seen against the backdrop of the snowy Alps. The moderating effect of the water itself and the skills of gardeners combine to make this possible.

OPPOSITE The terraces of Isola Bella rise sheer from the surface of Lake Maggiore. Man's power over nature is confirmed by his softening of the architectural surfaces with shaven greenery. God's creation forms the noble background, keeping us in our place.

away, the Borromean islands have always been locally owned, and the standard of horticultural achievement is as high as any you will find across the world.

Part of the delight of this garden world for the visitor is surely variety. Some of the people who made these Italian Lake gardens were princes, others foreign grandees or private individuals looking to make a personal paradise. Some gardens are ancient and richly overlaid with allegory and symbolism. Others are political gestures of the Napoleonic era. Still others were created to enable practical use to be made of an awkward site. Some visitors are attracted by visions of winding walks through thickets of *Rhododendron*, or a wall of trained novelty *Citrus* cultivars, or simply of a place to enjoy breakfast served by somebody else under a little pergola framing a lovely view. And in all these places,

OPPOSITE The elaborate flower beds and spectacular ornamental trees of the Villa Táranto at Pallanza on Lake Maggiore were the dream of a rich foreigner who wanted to create a woodland garden in a peerless setting. His vision remains startling today.
ABOVE On the approach to Isola Madre from Lake Maggiore, the villa perches invitingly near the landing stage, with the planting schemes, rich in their mature variety, spread all around it.

each season, each year is different: earlier, later, wetter, drier. It does not really matter. As every garden-lover knows, there are always pleasant surprises wherever you go. And if you do not like what is in front of you, you could always gaze out at the view. You will never tire of that.

HOW TO USE THIS BOOK

Gardens of the Italian Lakes can, of course, be enjoyed in its own right from the comfort of your armchair, but if I have done my job it will instil a desire to go and visit these places yourself. The gardens described are grouped into geographical regions, and each chapter is devoted to an individual garden. My aim is to reveal the garden's character by explaining how it was made and by whom, so that the reader can compare those formative intentions with what is there now. There is a lot of pleasure to be derived from walking in the makers' footsteps.

Although the area covered by this book is not large and is well served by various modes of transport, it would be something of a heroic effort to visit the whole lot in one go. It would be better to read and reflect on the locations and style of each garden and draw up your own itinerary. There are location maps on pages 214–15, and contact details and opening arrangements are listed on pages 216–17.

LAKE MAGGIORE

PART ONE

LAKE MAGGIORE

This is a pleasure-seeker's destination for those who trundle up on the train from Milan, an hour's journey away, or for the mainly German-speaking crowds who swarm over the Alps in a pale modern imitation of Goethe's *Italian Journey*, perhaps hoping to find the truth of his poem which begins: 'Kennst du das Land, wo die Zitronen blühn?' [Do you know that country, where the lemons bloom?], which has as much currency in the German mind as Wordsworth's daffodils do in mine.

It was not always so, and it is still easy enough to experience peace and quiet on the lake for those who trouble themselves to come a little out of season or who seek out the many quiet corners of this beautiful place. Bishop Burnet, who came here in 1686, was powerfully impressed by Lake Maggiore, whose length he inflated in his description to 'six and fifty miles' (the reality is more like 64 kilometres / 40 miles), and eulogized it as a 'great and noble lake', which is entirely accurate. He drew the reader's attention to the 'great bay to the westward' which is marked on maps as the Borromean Gulf, and which remains the centre of attraction for visitors from all parts. 'There lies here two islands', he wrote, 'called the Borromean islands, that are certainly the loveliest spots of ground in the world, there is nothing in all Italy that can be compared to them.' Every tourist board website of today seems feeble measured against Burnet's ecstatic prose. His encomium fixed an idea in the British mind that this lake and its jewels were something which must be sought out by every traveller in Italy.

Lake Maggiore was known to the Romans as Lacus Verbanus, after the *Verbena* which grows wild on its shores in the summer months. It is formed from the valleys of two rivers. The main body of the lake, which begins in the Alps around Locarno, is part of the course of the Ticino, a sufficiently long river to have a Swiss canton named after it, and which flows out into the flat countryside beyond Arona, whence it winds lazily away through the Lombard plain towards the Po. The reason for the western bay is that the lesser river, the Toce, enters here, forming a big reed bed, and gives the lake its distinctive shape on a map. Almost the whole length of the lake is framed in wooded

OPPOSITE Looking across the Borromean Gulf on Lake Maggiore through a filter of greenery, the town of Pallanza on the Castagnola peninsula can be identified projecting south. Behind it, the mountains rise on the approach to Switzerland.

mountains, with medium-sized towns appearing at intervals along the shore, which is more suitable for settlement than the gorge-like flanks of Lake Como; villages are plentifully scattered along the winding roads higher up on the banks. The traveller can reasonably expect a decent dusting of snow on the peaks around the lake in spring, and from many locations the daunting crags of the Swiss Alps loom in the not-too-distant background.

The garden at Isola Bella over which Bishop Burnet enthused was the creation of the Borromeo family, who have been powerfully influential on this lake since the fifteenth century. The Borromeo gradually increased their power here, not least by controlling the twin castles of Angera and Arona on either side of the southern end of the lake. The family still own the islands of Isola Bella and Isola Madre as well as the magnificent castle at Angera, picturesquely sited on the cliff top, but its counterpart at Arona was lost in the dramatic events of 1796. In that year, Napoleon Bonaparte's revolutionary French army crossed the Alps and overran Lombardy in the first foreign adventure of his career. The castle at Arona put up stiff resistance until it inevitably fell,

and in consequence was reduced to rubble. Napoleon's suite held their victory celebrations on the platform at the top of the garden on Isola Bella.

The Lake Maggiore of today seems an unlikely setting for revolutionary events, but in the mid-nineteenth century it was at the heart of just such a movement. The reason for this was that the eastern shore of the lake is in Lombardy, while the western shore is in Piedmont, with the proverbial red dotted line running straight down the middle. Until 1859, Lombardy was Austrian territory, and, though the Austrians seem to have been competent administrators, the rising tide of national sentiment required that it be included in the new nation state of Italy. Various attempts were made

---

BELOW An early nineteenth-century engraving shows the view across Lake Maggiore from the Villa Ruscello, near Stresa, revealing (left to right) the three islands of Isola dei Pescatori, Isola Madre and Isola Bella.
OPPOSITE The triumph of the Borromeo family is illustrated in the amphitheatre on Isola Bella, with the unicorn leaping from the top of an adapted Mount Parnassus. Divinities, obelisks, staircases and vegetation emphasize the point.

to achieve this. One of the most spectacular was Giuseppe Garibaldi and his red-shirted volunteers leading a pleasure steamer from Sesto Calende north along the lake, towing a ramshackle flotilla of boats of every size and description, all piled with everything that could fire a shot, to attack the twin Maginot-like Austrian forts guarding the entrance to the little port of Laveno. This heroic gesture could never have been more than just that, but the psychological effect was to rouse patriotic fervour in native hearts and rattle the Austrians, so that final victory soon became merely a matter of time.

In the nineteenth century, the lake was a major destination for travellers from the north of Europe, largely in search of the fabled terraces of Isola Bella, with which some were enchanted and others not. It was typically a prodigious journey over the Alps to get here, with many favouring a visit to Domodossola, a little to the north-west, en route, to view its main square, which, then as now, looked like a stage set from a romantic opera. Others, particularly the prosperous

British in the second half of the century, came via Genoa at the end of a winter in the favoured climate of the Riviera. Spring on the lakes had an irresistible appeal.

This relative isolation made for a pleasant feeling of exclusivity for those could afford it. Before 1900, Lake Maggiore was a destination for crowned heads and plumed helmets, who either built their villas here or imposed themselves on those who had already done so. Queen Victoria famously stayed at the Villa Clara near Baveno in 1879, wisely accepting an invitation to stay from its owner, Charles Henfrey, who had made his fortune building the railway system in India. At the time of her visit, the house was clearly visible from the road, and gentlemen who had waited there for hours stood up in their carriages and raised their hats as the widow of Windsor obliged them by waving briefly from the balcony. The queen also amused herself by painting capable watercolours of the view across the bay to the twin peaks of the Sasso del Ferro, the mountain that looms over the ferry port of Laveno and which now features a hang-glider platform at the top, around which enthusiasts swirl like pterodactyls in the summer thermals. The spiky roofline of the red-brick house at Villa Clara still appears prominently on the shore through its now magnificently mature foreground of evergreen trees. Not everyone was impressed by the house: Richard Bagot wrote in 1905 that it 'resembles nothing so much as the Wimbledon or Putney house of a retired tradesman'. Oh dear.

The little town of Stresa formed a convenient gathering-point for some of these villas, such as that of the Duchess of Genoa, and gradually the hotels began to form a promenade there, so that it took on something of the character of a seaside resort. Across the bay, Pallanza on the favoured Castagnola peninsula became another fashionable resort with an international mixture of villa owners along the shore and in the woods. Here, an important nursery trade sprang

up to cater for the garden-makers' requirements, with the great firm of Rovelli particularly successful throughout the nineteenth century. The soil around the lake is acid, and thus ideal for azaleas (*Rhododendron*) and *Camellia*. This has led to a trade in growing such shrubs which still flourishes today, especially at Fondotoce.

In 1905, a great change took place in the social atmosphere around Lake Maggiore when the Simplon rail tunnel was completed, a huge engineering achievement at very considerable human cost. The arduous journey over the Alps was no longer needed, and the crowds could pour through on the train. The effect was immediate: the royal visitors evaporated as if overnight, and the hotels in Stresa and Baveno proliferated. Things were a little different at Pallanza, which achieved a marketing coup by persuading the *Orient Express* to make its little station a regular stopping-off place for those with larger wallets. It was here, for example, that

Neil McEacharn decided to disembark from that train, having read in *The Times* that the Villa Táranto was for sale.

Now that the crowds were here, the pleasure boats followed, and the familiar pattern of the season on the lake developed. Isola Bella is a short distance from the landing stage at Stresa, and its famous terraces are one of the great sights of the town. Isola Madre has the same relationship with Pallanza. In modern times, some of the villa gardens have become accessible to the public, such as the Villa Pallavicino near Stresa, which functions as a sort of wildlife park among its magnificent woods, and the Villa Táranto, that curious mixture of sensational arboretum and dubious structures reflecting the character of its maker, Neil McEacharn. For those who make the journey north into the Swiss end of the lake, the great garden attraction is the lovely little island of Brissago with its elegant villa surrounded by an immaculately kept botanic garden.

The climate on Lake Maggiore is a very interesting one. Everyone who visits the gardens here is immediately impressed with two things: the power and vigour of growth; and the range of garden flora from so many different parts of the world, all looking perfectly at home. This seems unlikely, given the situation in the foothills of the Alps. The reasons are several. There is plenty of sunshine – this being Italy – but plenty of rain too. The pattern is the same as on Lake Como, with most of the rain falling during spring, summer and autumn, while winters, though cold, are relatively dry and bright. Extremes of temperature are moderated by the

BELOW The little island of Isola dei Pescatori, garden-free but full of delights, seen from Isola Bella. On the distant shore is the lakeside resort of Baveno. The vast white granite quarry, much debated by visitors, spreads up the mountainside behind.

sheer size of the body of water: any visitor to the lake will have experienced that feeling of an inland sea. This equable climate keeps growth green and steady.

The acid soil is due to the underlying granite, which can be seen in the vast quarries overlooking Baveno. It is also full of minerals from the rocks which have gradually slid down from the mountains over millions of years. This combination of climate and soil conditions results in the amazing growth rate of trees in particular, from the towering groves of the Villa Pallavicino to the modern wonders of the Villa Táranto, where ludicrously prosperous specimens were planted as recently as the mid-twentieth century.

Nature is, however, not always so generous to gardeners. Big storms blow out of the Alps from time to time, such as the one that flattened hundreds of trees on Isola Madre and broke Apollo's lyre on Isola Bella in the summer of 2006, and the seven-minute tornado which caused complete devastation in Pallanza in August 2013. Floods, too, are a recurrent menace, witnessed by small flood-height notices way above head height on lakeside buildings, and the images

TOP In the hill country north of Varese, the sixteenth-century garden of the Villa Cicogna Mozzoni transports the mind back to an age of courtly formality. Everyday life continues, now as then, just over the hedge.
ABOVE Many of these gardens are platforms for admiring the surrounding scenery. At the Villa San Remigio, a garden made by two artists, a picture frame built into a screen wall reveals a view of wooded mountains above Intra.

of waves sloshing over promenades in October 2014. The mind struggles to envisage the quantity of additional water required to raise the level of so vast a lake so very high. For all this occasional drama, Lake Maggiore remains an easy-going destination. The best way to see it is undoubtedly from the deck of one of the public passenger boats, a superb service which glides frequently back and forth between the various landing stages, providing unbeatable views of the famous island gardens with the lake and mountains behind them. The towns along the shore are inevitably dependent on the foreign tourist trade, but, as elsewhere in Italy, local traditions are everywhere in evidence, and there is no shortage of, for example, excellent food and drink wherever you go. The surprisingly clean waters of the lake teem with delicious fish such as *lavarello* – the 'white fish of the lake' as waiters blandly translate it – and this is the land of risotto, beef, cheeses and game, especially in the autumn, all washed down with some of the world's best wines, including Gavi,

Roero Arneis, Barbera and Barolo – all Piedmontese natives. As is often the case, the most ordinary-looking hostelry can be the venue for a memorable meal, and there are plenty of smarter establishments.

A lot of the fun of garden visiting on this lake resides in the sheer variety. A morning on Isola Bella is one of state and parade among the terraces and statues, followed by lunch on Isola dei Pescatori, a matter of metres away, and an afternoon stroll through the informal green groves of Isola Madre among the multicoloured wildfowl, with *Camellia* in spring and magnificent bedding in autumn. To get away from the crowds, take the *funivia* [cable car] up to the rock garden on the mountainside at Alpinia, or view the recreated medieval garden on the ramparts of the sensational Borromean castle at Angera. Getting around is easy enough, and travel on the lake is a pleasure in its own right. A day or two's stay will soon breed an easy familiarity, but the longer you are here the better it will be.

BELOW The unnerving regularity of the seasonal bedding at the Villa Táranto, laid out in panels on a bowling-green lawn, looks towards the house. The forested hills and snowy peaks beyond form a powerful contrast.

ISOLA BELLA

THE BAROQUE GARDEN IS a deliberately overwhelming experience. Placing one on an island adds a new level of theatrical novelty. Isola Bella is accordingly hugely popular with the visiting public. It lies close to the friendly little resort of Stresa, whence glide the excellent public service boats bringing fresh crowds of admirers. This makes the garden one of the most visited in Italy, but as it is without the vast promenades and parkland of its cousins at Versailles or Sanssouci the visitor is unlikely to find a spot for reflective solitude. So it should be: this is a style and a space intended for festive crowds on splendid occasions. It needs the glitter of sunlight and the imaginary flourish of trumpets. When standing on the paved platform at the top of the pyramid, or rather ziggurat, of terraces and looking out over the pretty parterres to the lake rimmed with mountains, it is clear that this is an entertainment worthy of a Roman emperor.

It was not always so. The Borromeo family began to purchase parcels of land on the island in the second half of the sixteenth century, but their main interest still lay on the larger island of Isola Madre. The Isola Bella project began in earnest in 1630, when Carlo III Borromeo set out to transform that island into a spectacular layout with a villa at one end axially linked to a great terraced garden at the other; the whole scheme was intended to look like a great ship floating in the lake. He started as he meant to go on, changing the island's name from the unpromising Isola Inferiore to Isola Isabella, in honour of his wife,

Isabella d'Adda. Isola Isabella soon became Isola Bella, and nobody seemed to complain. The 'lower island' had become 'beautiful'.

There were certain practical difficulties, not least the unwillingness of the cottagers to sell up and make room for these fancy notions. Eventually, Carlo was obliged to compromise by working the triumphal approach round the back of the cottages and permitting them their ancient processional route on set days. His men of business were left to resolve the question of how to bend an arrow-straight axis of honour without any visiting dignitary noticing.

After this initial difficulty, things moved forward rapidly. The master builder began work on the garden terraces in 1631, and in the following year Giovanni Angelo Crivelli of Milan developed plans for the house. By 1634, the bones of the present garden were already in place, with soil being brought over from the mainland.

Things then went quiet until the next owner, Vitaliano VI Borromeo, restarted the project, calling in Francesco Maria Ricchini to inflate the proposed villa into something more palatial. It is at this point that the crowd of names associated with the scheme begins to get out of hand, so it is worth considering Vitaliano's remark in a letter of 1686 that 'those constructions were all thought out by me, and as regards the inventions and ideas therein, I followed my genius'. The spirit of Louis XIV is apparent in these remarks, and we need not doubt Vitaliano's reliance on a succession of designers, artists and craftsmen to achieve the effect he wanted. He clearly supplied those necessary ingredients – commitment and money.

From 1650 onwards, the present appearance of the garden took shape. The obelisks and statues began to appear,

OPPOSITE Ancient and modern combine as Icelandic poppies (*Papaver nudicaule*) sprout among the gesticulating statues on Isola Bella. This happy blend is the key to the garden's enduring reputation. The lake and mountains contribute a share of desirable mystery.

giving life and detail to the silhouette. In 1659, Francesco Castelli took over as architect, again expanding the house. Garden detail progressed apace, with a hundred clay pots, each bearing the Borromeo crest of the three linked rings, commissioned in 1663.

The final push came with the arrival of Andrea Biffi as architect in 1671. His great contribution to the garden was to devise the Atrium of Diana, an octagonal space entered from the tapestry gallery of the house and rising via twin curving staircases into the garden. The kink in the axis of honour is placed in this space, but no visitor notices it because of the ingenious method of approach. Edwin Lutyens used a similar device to resolve the same difficulty in two of his English gardens in the early twentieth century.

Vitaliano VI permitted his self-confessed genius to be advised by some of the big names of the age, but apparently without significant effect. The sculptor Gian Lorenzo Bernini was sounded out in Rome, while the architect Carlo Fontana, tutor of, among others, Johann Bernhard Fischer von Erlach and James Gibbs, made some proposals for decoration in the house. However, the existing design represents the gradual realization of the original great project, essentially unaltered in its main lines.

From the beginning Isola Bella achieved its intended fame as a place of resort. Bishop Burnet, who left England in a hurry when James II came to the throne, relieved his boredom by touring Europe in 1686, when he visited Isola Bella and gave us our first detailed description. He was overwhelmed by what he saw, gushing that: 'The Borromean islands . . . are certainly the loveliest spots of ground in the World, there is nothing in all Italy that can be compared to them, they have the full view of the lake, and the ground rises so sweetly in them that nothing can be imagined like the Terrasses here.' He then remarked on the form of the terracing, the role of the two towers – one of which served to raise water from the lake to power the fountains – and the architectural nature of the plantings, with sweet oranges (*Citrus sinensis*) and citrons (*C. medica*) trained against the walls. He also mentioned a 'Great Parterre' in the French fashion, demonstrating that the current of design was flowing back into Italy from France. The fountains 'were not quite finished', leaving us to wonder what

BELOW Stout lads row a party of pleasure-seekers away from Isola Bella in an engraving of 1834. The house dominates one end of the island, and the famous terraces the other. Already the clean lines of the baroque garden are being softened by free-growing trees.

they might have been like, since little of the kind survives now. 'When all is finished', he continued, 'this place will look like an inchanted Island. The freshness of the Air, it being both in a Lake and near the Mountains, the fragrant Smell, the beautiful Prospect, and the delighting Variety that is here make it such a Habitation for Summer, that perhaps the whole World hath nothing like it.'

Bishop Burnet's is the authentic voice of the contemporary man of taste, and much of what he said rings down the ages to the sympathetic ear of the modern visitor. It is just that unique combination of swagger, scenery and brilliance which sums up Isola Bella's enduring appeal.

Many visitors have since visited Isola Bella and recorded their impressions, each influenced by the taste of their day. The French politician Charles de Brosses came in 1739, and predictably made disparaging remarks about the garden compared with examples from home, but still thought the place 'a little bit of fairyland, and [it] looks as if a portion

of the Garden of the Hesperides had been wafted to this enchanted spot'. Even by his visit, the garden fountains had dried up, though those in the series of grottoes in the house still functioned, and pleased him.

A defining event in the garden's history took place in 1797, when Napoleon Bonaparte took over the island for two days with his retinue. While there, he held a party on the great rectangular platform at the top of the garden, to celebrate the conquest of Lombardy.

During the nineteenth century, the northern European visitor began to find Isola Bella overrated. The essayist William Hazlitt thought his visit (in the rain) a waste of time: 'We were . . . utterly disappointed in the Isles Borromées', and he thought that the pictures in the palace were 'trash'. Things were much worse, however, for the political writer Samuel Laing in 1842. For him the island was:

> a monument of senseless expenditure . . . it is as bella as a rocky islet in a lake can be, covered entirely with parterres, and flower-pots, and grotto work, shell work, moss work, statuary work, and such gewgaws, with a French chateau to correspond. The isle so decked out amidst

ABOVE The terraces of Isola Bella, facing the promenade at Stresa, stack up like a tiered cake. This impression is heightened by the vertical accents of obelisks and statuary. The twin octagonal towers once drew up water from the lake.

scenery of a totally different character, looks
like an old court lady arrayed in silks, lace, and
diamonds, a hooped petticoat, and white satin
shoes, left by some mischance, squatting down all
alone in the midst of a Highland loch.

Another writer with a low opinion of Isola Bella was Richard
Bagot, who published his highly successful book *The Italian
Lakes* in 1905. Unlike our previous visitors, Bagot knew
the region intimately and gave tourist opinion short shrift.
He, too, took a dim view of the garden, and dismissed
the house entirely, but we see in his account the growing

RIGHT Lemons (*Citrus × limon*) and citrons (*C. medica*) in big terracotta
pots, bearing the Borromeo emblem of three linked rings, have
decorated the garden terraces for centuries. Their regular spacing along
the balustrades provides the stately rhythm of the baroque garden,
green and grey.

OPPOSITE ABOVE Facing the great terraces, the crowd of detail can be gradually teased out into its elements: emblematic statues of the seasons, a clever mixture of formal and informal planting, and an elaborate box (*Buxus*) parterre along the base.

ABOVE An astonishing sight from a window of the house is the private family lawn adorned with seasonal bedding of uniquely rococo beauty, picked out against mosaic-work spelling out the family's audacious motto, 'Humilitas'. There is much to reflect on here.

appreciation of the English-style plantings which had begun
a century before. Bagot disliked the baroque work, but was
comforted by informal plantings and the elevating effect
of the setting: 'The gardens are a triumph of bad taste . . .
the vulgarity of the whole conception is redeemed by the
luxuriance of the semi-tropical vegetation, which, owing
to the extreme mildness of the climate, flourishes in these
islands, and by the beauty of the views across the lake, to be
enjoyed from every angle of the terraces.'
Bagot's mixed opinions mark the turning point in the change
of attitude to Isola Bella in the twentieth century, from

ABOVE With green architecture all around, the shimmering tails of the
long-established flock of white peacocks catch the eye at every turn.
Their introduction in the seventeenth century was a stroke of genius
which continues to define the character of the garden.
RIGHT At every point, the calculated stiffness of the architecture is
interrupted by statues waving and leaning this way and that, and by the
comfortably rounded overlay of trees and shrubs which subtly brings the
garden up to date.

lined in cobble mosaics, and affording lovely framed views of the mountains and Isola dei Pescatori. There is also the glimpse over one of the private lawns adorned with Prince Borromeo's gasp-inducing motto 'Humilitas', with inevitable coronet above, scrolled out in delicate rococo seasonal bedding on the green lawn. This is a taste of things to come. After emerging from the tapestry gallery into the curious outdoor space of the Atrio di Diana, the visitor reaches the anteroom of the principal garden. This paved courtyard is the device which enabled Biffi to kink the desired straight axis from house to garden without anyone noticing as they leave it via a double staircase which permits no view behind or before. This also heightens the sense of arrival as the visitor enters the great garden space walking steadily upward and therefore a little out of puff, as they should be when entering a great man's personal paradise.

In fact, the major object to catch attention at the point of arrival is the giant spreading camphor tree (*Cinnamomum camphora*) on the immediate left. This gets variously written up as hugely ancient, but was in fact planted from a pot

in 1819 as part of the gradual attempt to overlay the new fashion of English informality on to the geometry of the baroque. This softer backdrop of irregular plantsmanship has come, perhaps surprisingly, to complement the earlier pomp and circumstance, and the happy balance between the two styles surely underlies the revival in public esteem of this famous garden during the twentieth century.

Beyond the camphor tree, the full effect of the original design begins to impose itself. The visitor steps up again to the amphitheatre, a baroque variation on Mount Parnassus, that is to say, a hill populated by Apollo and his attendants, the nine Muses. Here the hill is shallowly dished into a stacking set of niches, each inhabited by a statue and variously squirting jets of water. On the top, the ancient image of Pegasus has been adapted into the Borromeo device

BELOW The arcaded retaining walls of Isola Bella are a marvel in their own right, combining beauty with utility. Their regular pattern is echoed in the planting along the top. Behind, *Rhododendron* and tall pines frame the ever-twittering aviary.

TOP The big terracotta pots were originally made in Tuscany in 1663. Their successors continue to come from the same area.

ABOVE The visitor enters the garden from the house via the Atrio di Diana, an octagonal space designed to disguise the kink in the desired straight line of convention. The effect is achieved through the curving staircases rising from either side.

RIGHT The great 'amphitheatre' which greets the visitor on walking into the garden is a dramatic giant dished niche of niches. It is inhabited on several levels by various minor divinities and some magnificent scallop shells, a few of which spout fine jets of water.

of a giant unicorn rearing up, flanked by Apollo with his lyre and his counterpart Cybele.

Having climbed up to the highest level, the visitor now stands on the platform at the top of the pyramid of terraces. This paved entertaining space, still used for family wedding receptions, gives views out to the mountains and the lake through a forest of statues and obelisks. Many of them, though moderately formed of plain material, carry wonderfully delicate topknots of wrought iron in the forms of plumes and the various attributes of the deities, silhouetted against the sky. The views down over the richly planted parterres, walks and lawns are thoroughly rewarding,

OPPOSITE The pattern of the parterre is interestingly halfway between the geometry of Italian tradition and the scrollwork of its French successor. Within the spaces, the groundwork is coloured with crushed brick. Big pots of *Citrus* provide vertical accents.

ABOVE The collection of *Citrus* species and cultivars trained against the terrace walls has been famous here since the earliest records. The range and quality of the planting, and its maintenance to a superb standard, reflect the skills of the garden staff here.

and uniquely diversified by the improbable flock of white peacock – descendants of birds that have strutted here since the seventeenth century.

Those who grumble, sometimes with justification, about the poor quality of garden maintenance in Italian gardens will fall silent here. The standard is exemplary, the plant collection admirable at every season, and the bedding of such excellence, and different every year, as to convert the hardened cynic. There are many pleasures for those who seek them out: the age-old pattern of *Citrus* trees trained against the terrace walls; the view of that elegantly twin-peaked mountain, the Sasso del Ferro at Laveno, framed by big terracotta pots of *Plumbago*; the disarming hush of the gothic glasshouse; and the realization that all the plants are produced in the island's nursery.

Isola Bella has thrilled many and left others cold over the centuries. Its unique layout and character are intact, overseen by a dynamic and symbiotic combination of family pride, horticultural excellence and visitor income. Its reputation as a must-see destination is thoroughly deserved.

ISOLA MADRE

Half the fun of visiting Isola Madre lies in the approach. The great passenger boats rumble across the lake towards the island, slackening their speed as they near the landing stage. This gives pleasure-seekers on the foredeck the opportunity to read the composition in front of them. The villa, large and plain, presents its rectangular front at the top of the picture, thinly screened by palm trees, oleanders (*Nerium*) and climbers. Below it, several big terraces descend towards the visitor, one of them covered entirely, like a green render, in the foliage of the creeping fig (*Ficus pumila*). But best of all is the vegetation scattered along the rocky shore, where romantically tilted outcrops of slaty grey rock sprout curtains of pink and green, with the giant rosettes of variously coloured *Agave* hanging out over the lapping waves. As an overture, this is hard to beat, and, like all good overtures, it sets the tone for what is to come. The crown of a silver-grey gum (*Eucalyptus*) leans elegantly over the staircase as the visitor climbs on to the first terrace past massed bedding, always of the first quality, and steps into this floral wonderland through the pedimented arch.

The whole island is taken up with the garden and house. Nothing could be more different from the atmosphere on the sister island of Isola Bella, just a short distance away. There, all is splendour, nobility, state and parade. This, by contrast, is carpet slippers and afternoon tea. Both are unmissable, but the order in which they should be seen is quite clear. Some visitors feel that the crush and blaze of Isola Bella is such a knockout blow that it quite does them in, so they skip Isola Madre for a lie down in a darkened room. How wrong they are.

What is seen now in a walk around Isola Madre is the result of a series of modifications over many centuries. The lasting impression is of a richly planted ornamental garden in the English taste, laid out like soft furnishing over and around a thoroughly Italian framework of steps, clean lines and regular rhythms. The combination is a very happy one, with neither format quite gaining the upper hand, so that honour is retained on both sides. Above all, in this happy mingling of contrasting styles, the real victor is the view, framed at intervals across the dark blue lake to mountains, promontories, other islands and lakeshore promenades. It is easy enough here to find a quiet corner to contemplate the scenery and gather thoughts.

The island is on at least its third name so far. In the ninth century, it was named after San Vittore, a big saint in these parts, whose ancient chapel, now lost, stood here. A century later it was changed to Isola Maggiore, the 'bigger' or 'main' island, reasonably enough in comparison with the others. It has only been Isola Madre, the 'mother island', since 1713, and nobody really knows why. The island came into the Borromeo family in 1501, when Lancillotto Borromeo added it to the family's possessions. By 1542, it was covered with 550 grapevines (*Vitis*), with smaller plantations of walnuts (*Juglans*), figs (*Ficus*), olives (*Olea*), chestnuts (*Castanea*), cherries (*Prunus*), quinces (*Cydonia*), pomegranates (*Punica*) and apples (*Malus*). This interesting combination of fruits of both north and south shows that the accommodating qualities of the lake's climate were already appreciated. Before long, the family realized this might be an ideal spot for a summer residence with ornamental grounds, so that

OPPOSITE With its *Hibiscus* and palm trees surrounded by an Alpine lake, anyone who wishes to understand the mystery of how to grow the flora of an exceptional range of climates perfectly happily in the open air should begin their studies on Isola Madre.

by 1568 the owner has 'built a sumptuous palace, and ornamented it with an agreeable garden'. Pheasants make their first appearance in 1591; decorative terracing is added five years later. Already, by 1600, things are beginning to look the way they do now.

In the seventeenth century, all the action was concentrated on the big push of the Isola Bella project, and Isola Madre was left to its rural seclusion. Occasionally, it is mentioned in passing, and we realize that this apparent rustication is not quite what it seems: Conte Federigo Borromeo was accused in 1769, for example, of having a secret and inexhaustible source of wealth, so great was his expenditure on the estate, though this may have been idle flattery. The more telling remark seems likely to have been Carlo Amoretti's in 1794, when he observed that the gardens were subdivided into groves of wood, collections of trees, and orchards. This steady evolution from a productive estate to a pleasure ground can easily be felt by any modern visitor.

The final chapter of this extended makeover was written in the first half of the nineteenth century. Just as Isola Bella's character was gradually adapted at that time from a 'stone garden' of grey and green to a more varied backdrop of planting in tune with the rise of Romanticism, so Isola Madre was finally transformed into a plantsman's paradise, in which the foreign visitor could step ashore and imagine himself – like Joseph Banks in the South Seas – walking through groves of unfamiliar trees and shrubs with exotic birds wandering innocently across his pioneering path. This new style, suited to the changed mentality which valued individual specimens over the pictorial scenery favoured by the previous generation, was begun under the expert management of the Rovelli family, a famous name in these parts. Two brothers, Alessandro and Giuseppe, began their great work here in 1802, and the family remained successively head gardeners until 1851. Thereafter, they ran a highly successful nursery at Pallanza on the nearby shore.

ABOVE An engraving of 1834 reveals the villa on Isola Madre still starkly outlined above its regular terraces, but behind the house the groves are beginning to take on the looser form described with enthusiasm by later garden visitors.

By 1835, the character of the planting had been established. In that year, the Irishman Matthew O'Conor visited Isola Madre on his holiday trip through Europe, and was impressed not only by the international flora all thriving in the same spot, but also by the way the Italians, hitherto regarded as slaves to stony geometry, had mastered the art of informal planting: 'You ascend through groves of orange and lemon trees; no plant or shrub here seems to feel a foreign soil. The tea, Indian rubber, breadfruit, cotton, and pine-apple trees, and the lofty cedar of Lebanon, appear to have been planted there by the hand of nature.'

By this time, visitors were beginning to appreciate that the island was worth adding to their itinerary once they had visited famous Isola Bella, which was meanwhile declining in visitor esteem. Probably, many of them were put off by the extra half-hour's rowing time, but those who came tended to appreciate the relative quietness of Isola Madre, where they could have the place pretty much to themselves. From the middle of the century, this idea of strolling in an informal garden beyond the reach of the everyday world of commerce and government brought famous faces to the island. The young French novelist-to-be Gustave Flaubert

ABOVE A lake steamer pulls away from Isola Madre in a postcard view c.1905. The house is now framed in a landscape of mature trees and shrubs, with the terraces much less conspicuous. The mountains are dusted with snow.

BELOW The modern approach reveals the house rising from a picturesquely rocky shore overlooking ancient terraces festooned with exotic garden vegetation from many lands. An ideal balance of trees and shrubs, bedding and naturalized seedlings of every kind is at home here.

found himself on holiday here with his parents and sister in the spring of 1845, an adventure quite different to his usual earthier pursuits. These latter were perhaps not far from his mind when he wrote that he found Isola Madre the most 'voluptuous' location in the bay, with 'a thousand strange seductions', where he found himself in a 'sensual state'. The mind boggles.

Flaubert's compatriot Hippolyte Taine came in April 1864 and was powerfully impressed. We might expect baffling prose from the great philosopher, but he was instead poetically descriptive:

> . . . this is Isola Madre enwrapped in its terraces,
> the waves beating against its great blue stones
> and sprinkling its lustrous leaves with moisture

RIGHT A constant pleasure on Isola Madre is the agreeable contrast between the clean lines of the architecture, with long ramps leading to elegant gates, and the noble ease of the framing planting. Here, tall bamboo and billowing tree crowns do the job.

. . . . Aloes with their massive leaves and the Indian fig on the sides of the ledge are waving their tropical growths in the sunshine; avenues of lemon trees wind along the walls . . . the isle consists of a tuft of verdure expanding its masses of leaves above the water, laurels, evergreens, planes, pomegranates, exotic shrubbery, *Wisteria* and blooming clusters of azalea. One walks along surrounded by coolness and perfume; there is no one but a custodian; the island is deserted, seemingly awaiting some youthful prince and his fairy bride to screen their nuptials; thus carpeted with tender grass and flowery shrubs it is simply a lovely morning rose, a white and violet bouquet around which hover the bees . . . peacocks and pheasants quietly parade their golden robes starred with eyes or coated with purple, the undisputed sovereigns among a population of twittering and frolicsome birds.

Although things have changed somewhat since 1864, and the visitor can expect to find others there besides the custodian,

OPPOSITE Light and vegetation combine to produce rich effects, as here when the tall stems of the yellow bamboo *Phyllostachys sulphurea* f. *viridis* 'Mitis' are backlit against the form of a tree.

ABOVE The tone is set as soon as the boat arrives at the Isola Madre landing stage. Pots of seasonal bedding in thoughtful colour schemes are worked into the building fabric. *Aloe* and *Agave* in full glory are suspended above the rocky shore.

BELOW The brilliant colours of water lilies (*Nymphaea*) shine out from a nursery pool for the admiration of visitors at the café now occupied by the former orangery.

Taine's experience is immediately recognizable as the forerunner of what is seen now. The garden's new status on the bucket list of the illustrious was cemented in 1879, when both Umberto I, king of the newly unified nation of Italy, and Queen Victoria visited, though they took care to arrive on separate occasions.

After stepping off the boat today, the visitor is silently encouraged to follow an arrow-marked route. It is a good route, and shows the various scenes to best advantage on a gentle walk uphill to the house. It begins in a narrow defile between the rocks and the shore, ingeniously lined with exotic trees and shrubs, many from Australia. The visitor soon gets the idea that this is a rock outcrop in an ideal climate with plenty of sunshine and plenty of water, with the extremes of summer heat and winter cold moderated by the surrounding lake. In this happy compromise, plants from a vast range of different habitats across the world gather and dwell quite happily side by side, often expressing their pleasure by seeding themselves into a nearby crevice and growing to blowsy perfection in a way that no gardener other than God could hope to achieve.

This idea is soon illustrated when an unexpectedly shady stretch is reached, where water trickles down the face of an impossibly picturesque series of rocky ledges. All around is cool greenery, with ferns everywhere, both naturalized and

BELOW The chapel garden on Isola Madre is a neat and delicate set piece around an elliptical pool. The chapel itself, built to Defendente Vanini's design in 1858, bears pretty terracotta panels by Andrea Boni. The former orangery forms part of the same block.
OPPOSITE ABOVE A container of *Begonia* and *Gaura* in front of the villa looks out over the view south along the lake, framed by palms.
OPPOSITE BELOW Isola Madre affords many opportunities for quiet reflection. Here, decorative ironwork rails form the foreground to a panoramic view of the promenade across the lake at Pallanza.

in big pots. The chief pleasure is in the sight of the *Hosta* which obviously went native a long time ago, threading its way along the fissures in the rock, surely at least as happy here as it would be at home in faraway Japan. This is as good gardening as you will see anywhere in the world, and yet few visitors travelling to Italy dream of seeking out the cool and dripping recesses of artificial nature. There is constant variety along this route. At one point all is order, where seasonal bedding, always of excellent quality, is interrupted by ornamental trees, including a good specimen of *Davidia*

ABOVE Though the layout and planting are derived from British woodland gardens, the power of the Italian sun means that *Rhododendron* produce far more flowers in proportion to leaves than they do further north.
RIGHT The exotically reflexed blooms of *Gloriosa superba* 'Rothschildiana', despite being native to southern Africa, seem entirely at home in the floral wonderland of Isola Madre.

involucrata, completely festooned in gentlemen's white handkerchiefs in mid-spring, all against a backdrop of a long row of *Coleus*. Most of us are used to seeing the latter as a beginner's windowsill pot plant and it seems astonishingly magnificent at full scale, with every conceivable foliage colour variant on display along the wall. Many visitors must feel that they take the plant seriously for the first time when they meet it here.

The mood changes again as the boathouse is approached, where a gondola-like craft of great age is slung from the ceiling. From here, a lovely view is framed across to the

RIGHT A Dog of Fo guards the base of a staircase in the chapel garden. The walls are entirely covered in the foliage of creeping fig (*Ficus pumila*), which thrives on the Italian Lakes and responds happily to clipping.
BELOW Richly coloured water lily (*Nymphaea*) flowers mingle with tall *Cyperus* in a pool rimmed with *Begonia* below the staircase, in this characteristic scene on Isola Madre in which architecture and water blend with perennial and seasonal planting.

length of the promenade at Pallanza, with the Castagnola peninsula rising behind, topped by the Villa San Remigio. A great hedge of *Camellia* is the backdrop, never more beautiful than in early spring when a great carpet of squashy red flowers lies at its foot. The wise gardeners are in no hurry to clear it away.

A little beyond comes a rock garden full of charmers, intelligently planted so that there is plenty to admire in autumn as well as spring. Then comes the alarming-sounding *prato dei gobbi* [lawn of hunchbacks], so-called because of the woody 'knees' projecting up through the grass from the roots of a big swamp cypress (*Taxodium distichum*), a long way from its native home among the mangrove swamps of Florida. The knees (pneumatophores, if you wish) allow the roots in the wild to breathe under water, like a snorkel, and inevitably make mowing the lawn around the tree an unwelcome task.

To the right of the walk at this stage is a wall of evergreenery, largely bay laurel (*Laurus nobilis*), which grows

LEFT A giant *Eucalyptus* leans over an arched gate covered with neatly trimmed creeping fig (*Ficus pumila*). In the foreground, *Iresine* and *Begonia* combine to good effect in a pot.

BELOW A quiet path meanders past a collection of ornamental Japanese maple (*Acer japonicum* and *A. palmatum*) cultivars, their crowns thinned to allow light to reach the bulbs planted in the grass beneath.

superabundantly here. A few gaps are all that now show of
the immense damage caused by a storm that hit the island
at the end of June 2006, roaring out of the Alps to cut a
motorway-like swathe along this side of the island, and
flattening everything in its path. The amazing recovery of the
vegetation is once again testament to the prevailing growing
weather here.

It is at this point that the visitor is likely to notice, at first
out of the corner of one eye, the movement on the ground.
A quick double-check will confirm that it is an ornamental
fowl, perhaps the ridiculously brilliant, multicoloured Lady

ABOVE The collection of ornamental trees on the island, informally
grouped in the English style, includes many wonderful specimens
carefully planted to create contrasts of form and colour. Here a
five-needle pine and a grotesquely weeping cedar (*Cedrus*) lead the eye
to a flowering cherry tree.

Amherst's pheasant or the grandly distinguished silver
pheasant (black and white with red highlights) wandering
in and out of the shrubberies and across the dappled lawns.
This is all part of the deliberate contrast with the sister
island of Isola Bella, with its surreal colony of pure white
peacocks. On Isola Madre, the birds are as multicoloured as
the imagination can conceive and lead a charmed life in their
island paradise. Their numbers are predictably concentrated
around the aviary a little further on; although partly
demolished by that same storm, it was carefully restored
within weeks.

The very next object on the route is the house. When I first
saw it some years ago, it was something of a surprise. In the
courtyard immediately in front stood an immense Kashmir
cypress (*Cupressus cashmeriana*), so vast that the enormous
house behind it was completely invisible. This famous tree
arrived as a seed from a Borromeo-sponsored plant-hunting

expedition in 1862. It is easy enough to imagine its elegant young form in the centre of the courtyard, with its weeping, blue-green branches the very cynosure of mid-nineteenth-century garden taste. Nobody could have expected that it would achieve such monumental dimensions, still less that it would retain its unique appearance. It was a famous object and the pride of this place. But the great storm of 2006 blew it flat. It might have been worse, because if the Kashmir cypress had landed on the house, that would have been that. The monster lay on the ground like Goliath, surrounded by cries of disbelief and despair. But then Prince Borromeo decided it could be saved, lying there, like many trees do when blown over, attached by a hinge of the rootplate on one side. So he hired a helicopter, which attached a cable to the fallen tree and pulled it upright. Further cable-braces were then stretched out on all sides as if it were an enormous flagpole. Now this is all very splendid and marvellous, not to say unheard-of, but my immediate reaction was that it would all end in failure, since conifers cannot regenerate

their severed limbs. However, as the years go by, the tree has gradually regained its glory, and I am obviously wrong. Having said that, all the steel cables are still in place, and it is difficult to imagine the day when they can safely be removed. Rounding the house at this point, the visitor comes to one of the highlights of the garden – the little square flanked by the chapel and filled by an ornamental pond. They can look down from a staircase on to this elliptical pond, planted with multicoloured water lilies (*Nymphaea*), including some of the exotically coloured Latour-Marliac types, and edged with bedding of the kind that the Borromeo gardens do so well, whatever the season. Straight ahead is an iron pergola planted with *Wisteria* in a style which could happen only in

BELOW Where the handsomely mossy roots of a big tree spread out against the path, mondo grass (*Ophiopogon japonicus*) flourishes where no true grass could. Rising from its mat are tree ferns (*Dicksonia antarctica*) and bamboos, allowing a view through to the open lawns beyond.

Italy: three cultivars – pink, white and the familiar blue – in broad stripes. The effect is novel, and the scent in mid-spring overwhelming, as it drifts on the air. The chapel, built in 1858 and faced in terracotta panels, is a pretty thing, and still in use for family weddings and christenings. Joined on to it, but facing across the lake, is the former orangery, now, like so many of its kind, in use as a tea shop, in front of which chairs and tables are pleasantly shaded by a grove of bananas (*Musa*).

From here the visitor walks across the looming façade of the villa, festooned in late summer with curtains of *Bougainvillea*.

ABOVE LEFT Mature woodland-garden planting of an older generation finds *Rhododendron* in bloom over a ground cover of *Skimmia*, both revelling in the naturally acid, free-draining soil here.

ABOVE RIGHT Entrance stage right for a perfectly posed silver pheasant set against an appropriate backdrop of white daffodils. For those who have the patience to remain still and silent, this sort of theatrical scene is readily available on Isola Madre.

The bedding along its base is always magnificent and complements the lawns and those very palms which were first seen on arrival. At the end of this walk is a little showpiece, a collection of *Protea*, the national flower of South Africa, in pots. Overlooking them is a big maidenhair tree (*Ginkgo*), always a picture of health, as so many plants are here in this ideal climate.

The lawns and specimen trees and shrubs spread away in various directions beyond the house, continuing the *giardino inglese* impression which has been gathering on Isola Madre since the start of the nineteenth century. In modern times all this has been superintended by Gianfranco Giustina, head gardener here for more than thirty years. Since 2006, he has also been in charge, like a supreme allied commander, on Isola Bella. He sets the marvellous standard on these islands, and was awarded the Royal Horticultural Society's Veitch Memorial Medal in 2014, when the appropriately named Jim Gardiner travelled from RHS Wisley to Pallanza to present it. When a garden is this good, everyone is happy.

VILLA TÁRANTO

At the entrance to the Villa Táranto, just inside the imposing gates, is a very big tree. It is a specimen of scarlet oak (*Quercus coccinea*), one of those American species planted for its spectacular autumn colour. It is so big, so thick in the trunk, so healthy and vigorous that it cannot fail to impress on every front, despite being hemmed in by terracing and paving on every side. Each autumn, its carpet of acorns, though daily swept away, impedes the progress of those approaching the adjacent café. The visitor naturally assumes that it must be very old, certainly hundreds of years. For once, they need not speculate for long, since one of the good things about the garden here is that all the plants are clearly and informatively labelled. The label states that it was planted in 1938. Pause for a short period of incredulity. This tells a great deal about the favourable growing conditions on Lake Maggiore, and prepares visitors for the treats in store as they walk through this plant-lover's paradise. It also sets the mind racing on what other things were happening in Italy in 1938, and what was about to happen next.

An early shock is a good preparation here, for the garden at the Villa Táranto in Pallanza, beneath its shining surface, is a place of mystery and contradiction. On the one hand, it is one of the most magnificent collections of trees and shrubs in the world, with prize specimens everywhere, superbly maintained, easy to get to and with all the facilities any visitor could reasonably require. On the other hand, it is a faintly unnerving period piece leading the visitor through a compendium of startlingly ugly design features. Eventually, the good things win out, but the feeling that it could have gone either way lingers uncomfortably in the mind.

The source of the mystery probably lies in the personality of the garden's founding father, the enigmatic Neil McEacharn. The visitor is aware of him at every turn in the garden, so they naturally wish to know more about the great man, and there the difficulty begins. The received wisdom is that he was a Scottish sea captain, born at Galloway House, a member of the Queen's Royal Scottish Archers and a distinguished botanist. There are elements of truth in this, but anyone embarking on a conventional line of research will soon find themselves stumbling about in a fog of uncertainty. Nonetheless, the story, shorn of myth and rumour, goes broadly like this. Neil Boyd Watson McEacharn was born in London in 1884. His father was Malcolm McEacharn, also born in London, though of Scottish parentage, a brilliantly successful businessman who made his money and his name in Australia initially through the shipping line McIlwraith McEacharn Ltd ('The Scottish Line') by exporting frozen meat and butter to Britain. Malcolm became a powerful politician, received a knighthood and returned in triumph to his native land, establishing himself as a country landowner by purchasing the Galloway House estate. His second wife, and Neil's mother, was the daughter of John Boyd Watson, born in Paisley, who became immensely rich as a pioneer at the Bendigo gold mines in Victoria. It will be seen from this brief résumé that Neil McEacharn's personality was suffused with notions of Scottishness, that he was a thoroughly international character and that he had a lot of money at his disposal.

Neil McEacharn was interested in gardens from an early age. In the vast grounds of Galloway House, he could see the potential for a woodland garden in the fashionable style of the early twentieth century. Everything was in his favour: he had the drive, the money, and the site. Galloway, in the south-western corner of Scotland, is ideally suited to the cultivation of a wide range of plant species, being washed by the waters of the famous Gulf Stream, which makes so many things possible on both sides of the Irish Sea. Galloway House looks out over those very waters. Not far to the west is the justly famous botanic garden at Logan, where species thrive which can barely be persuaded to grow elsewhere in Britain. A woodland garden would be just the thing at Galloway House, where Neil McEacharn could vie with others from a similar background, like the Aberconways of Bodnant or the Armstrongs of Cragside. Also, this was the golden age of plant hunting, when new species ideal for European gardens were pouring in from the amazing expeditions of men such as Ernest 'Chinese' Wilson, whose trees, shrubs, perennials and lilies continue to thrill us today. But for all this golden opportunity, McEacharn hesitated.

Perhaps Galloway House was too far off the beaten track for a rich man of fashion wishing to cut a dash in this world; perhaps, for all its potential, the climate was too grey and wet for a well-travelled man who wondered if there might be somewhere with similar climatic advantages but rather more sun, and rather more of a convivial atmosphere – some happy medium combining the advantages of Scotland and Australia.

According to his own account, McEacharn was travelling on a train one day in 1930, reading *The Times*, when he saw the site of the Villa Táranto for sale. He made haste to Pallanza and bought it on the spot. Whatever the reality, McEacharn had bought a late nineteenth-century house, then called Villa La Crocetta, with a level garden around it, and a sweeping valley side running down to the shore of Lake Maggiore.

BELOW In spring, the lower garden is a heady mixture of dazzling bedding and a mingled overlay of delicately flowering trees and shrubs.

The large plot was on the edge of the polite lakeside resort of Pallanza, a residential suburb of the well-to-do along a distinctive, south-facing headland called the Castagnola peninsula, just where the Borromean Gulf joins the main body of the lake. Next door was the famous garden of the Villa San Remigio, the home of Sophie Browne (McEacharn knew her as Dida). The road into Pallanza around the headland was lined with handsome villas and select hotels, and the town boasted numerous illustrious residents, including Field Marshal Cadorna, commander of the Italian

army in the First World War, the sculptor Paolo Troubetzkoy and, on the little island of San Giorgio, the flamboyant conductor Arturo Toscanini. It is easy to see why McEacharn felt this was more like it. He promptly sold Galloway House to Lady Forteviot of the Dewar's Whisky dynasty, and embarked on his great new project.

Work began in 1930. McEacharn started by removing the parterre around the Villa La Crocetta, which is an unexpected object, decidedly French-looking, as if it had turned up like the Tardis from a polite suburb of the new Paris of Napoleon III. It is not known what the parterre looked like except for McEacharn's withering description of it in his book, in which he referred to 'badly-designed Italian formal gardens and endless dreadful statues'. I suspect it may be something of a loss, but the modern eye can only try to imagine it spread across the present level rectangular lawn, over which the house is viewed from a respectful distance through the mist

ABOVE In spring, billowing crowns of flowering *Prunus* and *Magnolia* form the foreground to the view over Lake Maggiore, with the peak of the Sasso del Ferro on the right.

OVERLEAF Panels of blue and yellow bedding interlock with the pools in the flower garden overseen by the little bronze boy. The house is in the middle distance, with the Swiss Alps beyond.

of a fountain, perhaps a descendant of the original. McEacharn had big ideas, and, having begun major plantings at Galloway House, he was keen to make progress. He secured extra plots of adjacent land to consolidate his new estate, and changed the name of the house to the Villa Táranto, apparently in commemoration of a distinguished military ancestor, thus adding to his growing air of an international man of mystery. What he now required was a horticulturist capable of carrying out the great project. Here he chose well. Henry Cocker, the son of a London doctor, had trained at Kew, and as part of his course had spent a year working at the internationally famous garden of the Hanbury family at La Mortola, near Ventimiglia, just where the Italian Riviera meets the French border. Cocker was looking for a flying start to his career when McEacharn and the Villa Táranto came along. It was the ideal combination. Cocker started at the Villa Táranto in 1933, when the heavy work of clearance and levelling was well advanced. It will never be known which of the two men was the greater

influence over what is seen now, but it was clearly a joint venture from the beginning. The idea was to create a private botanic garden of international significance, laid out in the manner of a British woodland garden. McEacharn made it clear at an early stage that he knew what he wanted, but that he had complete confidence in Cocker's judgment when it came to plant selection, placement and cultivation, and would back it with whatever financial and organizational arrangements were required. Cocker must have been equally thrilled and daunted by the opportunity, but he was the right man for the job.

BELOW The multiple jets of the fountain at the end of the double herbaceous borders inevitably attract the visitor's attention on the approach to the lower flower garden.
OPPOSITE Grey putti play in the fountain, enjoying that especially Italian phenomenon of glittering water. The magnificent, shield-like leaves of *Colocasia* revel in the combination of warmth and wet.

The garden rapidly took on its present form, with a set route along the valley bottom, opening out into decorative gardens, then rising to the platform of the house and beyond before gradually winding back down to the entrance. Though McEacharn made it clear that this was to be a private garden from the outset, its character is openly institutional, and he must have seen it that way in his mind. Clearance of

the 'uninviting mass' of existing vegetation proceeded under Cocker's steady eye, and the next five years must have been a period of monumental activity, since pretty well everything now seen was achieved in that short period. The record seems to speak of hundreds of labourers toiling under expert direction, and for once this seems entirely plausible. Cocker soon found that he had found the perfect setting in practical terms. The climate was bright and sunny; there was plenty of rain throughout the year; and the vast surface of the lake evened out the highs and lows of seasonal temperatures. Another decisive advantage was the topsoil, a rich dark acid material derived from the ancient bed of the lake, many metres deep in places and ideal for the *Rhododendron* forests that no doubt stretched away before McEacharn's imagination. All these factors provided growing conditions of which Cocker could only have dreamt elsewhere. It must have seemed to the owner that his head

OPPOSITE ABOVE Standards of *Lantana camara* rise above groundwork of busy Lizzie (*Impatiens*) near the Villino (the curator's house and library of the garden).

OPPOSITE BELOW An immense pool of the fabled sacred lotus (*Nelumbo nucifera*) lights up a terrace in the upper flower garden. Its leaves represent the rays of the sun, and its seed heads suggest an art nouveau showerhead.

ABOVE The pergola at the top of the garden is planted with *Wisteria*, hung with plump pods in the autumn, and the twining shoots of Kiwi fruit (*Actinidia deliciosa*).

gardener was the modern Joseph Paxton, able to conjure up success every time beyond anyone's reasonable expectation. Once the retaining walls, drains, irrigation systems and nursery were in place, the planting began, on a monumental scale and involving large-scale importation from all over the world. *Rhododendron*, often big specimens, were rootballed in Cornwall and loaded on to trains. Tree ferns, surplus to requirements in Australia but much admired in Europe, came by the route of the original McEacharn fortunes. Groves of birches (*Betula*) and *Hydrangea*, *Camellia* and *Magnolia* were rapidly established, all meticulously labelled and catalogued. Cocker marshalled his army of gardeners while McEacharn's lunch guests found themselves extracting seeds at tables set out by the windows of the villa.

The landform, meanwhile, was gradually altered to suit the vision. The cobbled road of neat setts, like a street in the middle of Munich, which winds through the garden was there from the start. The stone bridge across the valley was a major achievement of 1937, after the little valley had been widened, deepened and its sides graded to accommodate shade-loving plants. One of the best legacies of the early days is to be enjoyed here by walking across this bridge in spring next to the crowns of a group of *Paulownia* hanging their purple foxglove flowers over the parapet for the pleasure of the onlooker.

The visitor now sees the trees planted in this early phase of the garden in their magnificent maturity. The great mixed avenue of conifers leading into the garden from the entrance is a triumph which would have thrilled its makers: each specimen is perfectly placed with sufficient room to spread its full crown, the branches sweep right down to the ground all round, and everything is a picture of health and vigour. All was not well, however, in this private Eden. McEacharn and Cocker must have known from the outset that Europe in the 1930s was facing disaster, and things soon became

BELOW The expanding leaves and flowers of Santa Cruz water lily (*Victoria cruziana*), one of the giant water lilies of South America, populate the swimming-pool-blue waters in the upper flower garden. The immaculate garden world of a lost era lies beyond.

serious. The political difficulties grew steadily greater until finally, in 1940, the two of them were obliged to clear out or face internment as enemy aliens. Cocker just caught the last coal-boat back to England from Cannes. Its fateful voyage was described by Somerset Maugham in his memoirs. McEacharn also returned to London with his lady friend, a German princess whom he quickly married, to prevent her internment. He gradually found his way via Canada back to Australia for the duration of the Second World War.

The garden at Villa Táranto might well have been lost at this time but for two factors. The first was McEacharn's decision, perhaps under duress, to transfer the ownership of the Villa Táranto to the Italian state, reserving a life interest for himself. The second was the continued presence there of McEacharn's secretary, Dr Antonio Cappelletto, until the war was over. He is very properly commemorated alongside his master in the distinctive mausoleum. The danger for him must have been very great at times.

Despite everything, McEacharn and Cocker came back and carried on in 1947. Cocker had the joy of finally marrying his local love, who had been obliged to stay behind when he left seven years earlier. The garden continued to develop, including the addition of the double herbaceous borders

which any visitor soon encounters, surely the only ones in Italy and a testament to the absurdity of British gardening abroad. It is the horticultural equivalent of Brown Windsor soup on a Riviera hotel menu, and reminds me of Dr Johnson's remark about a dog standing on its hind legs. By 1952, McEacharn had persuaded himself, perhaps by inspecting his bank balance, that the paying public ought to be admitted to his botanical paradise. Big crowds arrived, and McEacharn uttered the time-honoured words of relief in these circumstances that they had caused remarkably little damage. From then on his reputation as a magnanimous grandee rose, so that we now lift our hats to his image or his tomb in various parts of the garden. If ever a garden were designed for great crowds this is it, complete with its own landing stage for the lake boats. A quarter of a million visitors come every year, filing in wonder along the endlessly winding tulip display in mid-spring, a feat of planting which can be beaten only by the same walk in early autumn, when planted with *Dahlia* 2.75 metres/9 feet high and covered with blooms from head to foot. Every species of gardener is catered for here.

The predominant style of display is that of the informal woodland garden, with great groves of specimen trees towering over groups of ornamental shrubs. But there any resemblance to a British equivalent, such as Dawyck in the Scottish borders, which is perhaps the garden ideal with which McEacharn set off, comes to an end. Here, each tree sits in its own little bed, the grass around it neatly shorn, and we can forget the notion of sheets of daffodils (*Narcissus*) or Himalayan blue poppies (*Meconopsis*) such as at Dawyck or the Savill Garden, Windsor. Nature here is kept under

ABOVE LEFT The shrubs here have many treats in store for the specialist. Here, *Franklinia alatamaha*, an American native now extinct in its former home, produces a perfect bloom to make us all reflect on the importance of such collections.

ABOVE RIGHT A spring planting of rich subtlety at the Villa Táranto. Here, the varying forms and colours of two tulip cultivars mingle happily with a multi-headed *Narcissus*.

strict control, with the greenest bowling-green lawns in the world on show at every turn. The bedding, too, in contrast to the beauties of the island gardens, is stiff and startling, favouring such blinding combinations at a vast bed of scarlet and yellow *Celosia*. Sometimes things are better, such as the 0.8 kilometre / ½ mile of *Primula obconica* on view one spring, but shock and awe tend to predominate over tender delicacy. This is a pity, because the woody collections are truly memorable. These are cleverly grouped, so that the visitor moves through a long walk of Japanese maple (*Acer japonicum* and *A. palmatum*) cultivars, each grown to perfection and accurately labelled – a perfect example of education and beauty in harmony.

The individual trees never fail to impress by their health and vigour. The founding fathers had the wit to leave a few specimens of the ancient wood-pasture sweet chestnut (*Castanea sativa*) pollards, one of which is ideally placed at a dividing of the walks, its great crown spreading nobly out over the thoughtful visitor. A little further on the walk up to the bridge, a huge handkerchief tree (*Davidia involucrata*) spreads its branches picturesquely down the slope. Each mid-spring, it is covered in spectacular white handkerchiefs (or doves, if you prefer). It looks for all the world as if it has been doing just that for centuries.

There is another handkerchief tree near the highest point in the garden. According to its informative label, it was planted by the Infante of Spain in August 1938. After wrestling with the bizarre notion of planting a tree in August in Italy, the mind soon realizes that this is the region of the garden given over to commemorative tree plantings by the great and the good. Now the broad winding road makes sense: we can visualize Konrad Adenauer, the long-lived Princess Alice, countess of Athlone, and other grandees being driven slowly through the garden in an open-topped car, expressing polite interest in their surroundings. Giulio Andreotti, seven times Italian prime minister, was a frequent visitor.

OPPOSITE The dramatic waving line of tulips draws the visitor into its seemingly endless parade, shifting colour combinations along its length, all labelled for the visitor's notebook.

ABOVE There is nothing on earth like the tulip display in spring at the Villa Táranto. In this section, mixed doubles in a heady combination of primary colours with lilac are bound to provoke a vigorous debate.

ABOVE If you were thinking of dozing off, this bed of mixed Icelandic poppies (*Papaver nudicaule*) and purple *Anemone* will give you the necessary pick-me-up.

Perhaps Andreotti was here, a little awkwardly, when Margaret Thatcher planted her tree. We can imagine her reaction to her specimen being positioned three rows back.

The modern wonder of the Villa Táranto is that it is there at all. The storm that caused such devastation at the Villa San Remigio in late August 2012 also did huge damage here. Of the 3,000 trees in the collection, a third were destroyed. I remember looking in through the gates a few days later and seeing the immense pile of sawn-up tree trunks piled up in the car park, and wondering whether this might be the end. In fact, the garden opened again the following spring as usual after a winter of furious activity clearing away the damage and beginning the process of repair and renewal. The most obvious sign of change is in the view near the bridge, where a huge institutional building dominates the view on the horizon. Before the storm it was completely hidden by trees, so that no one would have known it was there. Immense credit is due to the management and workforce for making the place look so marvellous in so short a space of time. It is superficial to say that these huge losses create new planting opportunities, but the rate of progress has been magnificent. The first-time visitor would be unaware of the damage, and the speed of growth here is so rapid that this great garden can look forward with confidence to a long and brilliant future. There is nowhere like it in the world.

LEFT Cherry (*Prunus*) blossom and daffodils (*Narcissus*) fill the brightly lit spring scene among the brilliant shaven lawns of the lower flower garden at the Villa Táranto. Strict order and blowsy ease are locked in a perpetual struggle for supremacy.

VILLA SAN REMIGIO

At the top of a quiet suburban lane in Pallanza stands a lovely little Romanesque church, its grey stones concealing ancient frescoes within. With an effort of the imagination it is still possible to see it as it must once have stood, alone on the high point of the Castagnola promontory, among the chestnut (*Castanea*) woods and fields of the district. Nowadays, it is flanked by two nineteenth-century villas, each of which is closely linked to our story of two lovers who made a garden of abiding sentiment here at the beginning of the twentieth century. The garden speaks for itself, but the story of how it came to be is worth hearing, and adds depth to our understanding of this special place.

In 1863, Peter Browne, a retired Anglo-Irish diplomat, came here on holiday with his three daughters. Browne was from County Mayo in the west of Ireland, where his family were close relatives of the Marquess of Sligo, whose great seat, Westport House, loomed a few kilometres from Mount Browne. Although Browne always acknowledged his roots, he was an absentee landlord just when Maria Edgeworth wrote her famous novel on that subject. He served for a time as Tory MP for Rye in Sussex, before embarking on what he expected to be a brilliant diplomatic career. He was soon posted to Copenhagen as British chargé d'affaires. This was rather a good posting, one would have thought, given some of the alternatives, but despite his letters

expressing his frustration to successive prime ministers, he remained there unpromoted for the rest of his thirty-year career. We need not worry, however, since his perceived loss of personal dignity must have been assuaged by his very substantial pension.

As Browne stood on the hill overlooking the little church that beautiful day in 1863, with glorious views unfolding over the Borromean islands, his daughters urged him to use his ample leisure and funds to buy the site and build a house on it. His resistance seems to have been slight, and he did just that, building a villa in the characteristic chalet-esque style of the period on the crown of the hill, a position boldly visible to this day to passengers on boats rounding the headland. The new house was filled with souvenirs of Peter's Danish service, and a garden began to cover the slopes falling away on all sides around the house. Browne's family spent their holidays here for many years.

Two generations later, the Browne presence was thoroughly entwined with the location. Though family members continued to be born in Dublin or London, there were at least two of Peter Browne's descendants living next to the little church. In 1866, Peter's granddaughter Sophie Browne was born, and on her father's death in 1883 she remained at the Villa San Remigio with her widowed mother, Emily. Meanwhile, across the lane, a second house, the Villino [little villa] San Remigio, had been built for another of Peter's daughters, Esther, who had married the Marchese Della Valle di Casanova. They had a son, named Silvio.

Little Silvio and Sophie were close friends from childhood, and constantly in and out of one another's house and garden. It could hardly have been otherwise. They were each of an artistic outlook: she as a painter, he as a poet and musician. As time went on, it became increasingly apparent that there was more to this than the childish friendship with which the two sets of parents would have been perfectly happy. Silvio and Sophie were in love, and wanted to get married. By the 1880s, however, the consequences of Darwinian thinking were beginning to become apparent, and the idea of first cousins marrying was badly received.

Despite the marital ban, the couple's burgeoning plans for something grander on the site gathered pace. From 1887, broad terraces began to be built down the slope from the house towards the lane, and a studio in the form of a chapel arose on the opposite flank. Beyond the terracing, the scheme broke out into naturalistic parkland in the English style, thinly scattered with ornamental trees, through which a long serpentine drive wound up the hill from a new entrance on the lake shore.

In 1896, Sophie's mother died, removing the last obstacle to her attachment. Within weeks, the neighbour-cousin-lovers married. It must have been quite a moment when Sophie Browne was suddenly transformed at the altar into La Marchesa Sofia Della Valle di Casanova. Now the brakes were off, and the full scheme unfolded rapidly. The garden

was a greater priority than the house, and this is indicated by a photograph of around 1900, which shows the garden in more or less its present form with Peter Browne's chalet intact at the top. That house was soon taken down, however, and replaced on the same site with something much grander – the Edwardian version of an Italian villa, which we see today. Silvio and Sophie filled the house with antiques, turning it into the sort of home of taste much favoured by Anglo-American expatriates in other parts of Italy at that time. There were gilt-framed madonnas and sets of ancient weaponry decorating the walls. Something of the sort can still be seen in the interiors of the Villa La Pietra, the former Acton family house on the northern outskirts of Florence.

It would be wrong, however, to pigeonhole Silvio and Sophie as mere wealthy aesthetes gradually filling their lovely home

BELOW A postcard c.1905 shows the scene much as it is today. The terraces and their decoration were then quite new. Peter Browne's chalet-like house of the 1860s was about to be replaced, and the mature trees in the background are perhaps also of his time.

OPPOSITE The view up to the house from the Garden of Sadness shows that, despite some ragged edges, the garden terraces are essentially intact. The broad staircases are offset by cast stonework of rococo delicacy, and walls are hung with creeping fig (*Ficus pumila*).

with antiques. They were much more determined and adventurous than that, and fully immersed in the artistic movements of their time. Sophie was an accomplished painter, and trained under Arnaldo Ferraguti, some of whose dramatic style can be seen in the lovely little Museo del Paesaggio [landscape museum] in Pallanza. In the same museum are several of Sophie's own pastels, as well as a sombre, full-length portrait of her as some melancholy Tudor heroine, perhaps Amy Robsart from Walter Scott's *Kenilworth*. Silvio was a German Romantic by inclination, but could never quite settle to one art form or another. He published poetry (in German), studied piano with Franz Liszt and left his collection of impressionist paintings to the city of Stuttgart, which founded its art gallery on that basis.

The Villa San Remigio became a significant salon for artists and writers from all over Europe, and it is pleasant to think of the many famous people who talked in its rooms and sat on its terraces during the glory years either side of 1900. The Danish philosopher Georg Brandes wrote home that he thought Silvio odd and Sophie wise, and the art critic

Bernard Berenson looked in on his search for great paintings, and perhaps compared the terraced garden with his own unfolding ideas for his home at I Tatti, near Florence. The Futurist Umberto Boccioni painted the composer Ferruccio Busoni leaning over a balcony at Villa San Remigio, with the garden gleaming behind him, while writers and personalities as different as Hermann Hesse and Gabriele D'Annunzio also came and went.

All this was the lively backdrop to the making of Silvio and Sophie's life's work – the new garden. On the face of it, this was an extension of the foreigner's interpretation of Italian ideas so often to be found in the Italy of that time, and to that extent a logical continuation of the house. Yet anyone walking round the garden cannot help but see that there is something much more mysterious going on here, something quite original and thoroughly romantic. Each of the terraces has its own theme, with a name and a style, and often there are poetic inscriptions to trigger the imagination. Any suggestion of drippy Edwardian tweeness, sometimes found in gardens of this date in England, is quite banished by the

continuing subtle undercurrent of quiet themes, reinforced by the powerful sense of two minds with a common purpose. Even the present state of crumbling decay adds to the atmosphere of pleasing melancholy.

It is best to start a visit at the foot of the terraces, which step down from the house towards the lane. The first of these gardens sets the tone for what is to come, and is quite unexpected. This is the Garden of Sadness. What on earth had these two to be sad about? They had enduring love, shared ideals, a wonderful site, money, ideas and lots of like-minded friends. But this is to misunderstand sadness: here it is silence, stillness, inward reflection, rooted in the

ABOVE Classical deities on top of tall slender gate piers stand at the head of the long drive, which winds up through parkland from the lake shore. The house, on top of the hill, is a clean-lined villa reviving an unspecified period of Italian architectural history.

LEFT A postcard of the 1920s shows how the ancient church tower was ingeniously worked into the garden layout. The view across the terrace reveals the strictly architectural approach, with cast stone and shaven greenery rising over gravel walks punctuated with occasional specimen shrubs.

German Romantic standing alone on the edge of a wood at dusk as the last notes of birdsong die away. This was, after all, a garden for which a model was made and viewed by moonlight to see if it felt right.

But how to express sadness in a garden? A little observation reveals the theme. There are no flowers here, just plain lawns, which early photographs show to have been left a little rough by infrequent mowing. In the lawns are rectangular pools with statues, but the expected fountains do not play, for this is the silent music of the mind. Most surprising of all is the non-view: the garden is ideally placed for a glorious prospect over the garden islands in the lake far below, but a screen of stone blocks out any view, acting instead as a niche for a statue of Hercules beating the Hydra to death with his club. There is, perhaps, also a practical reason for the screen, which prevents any view from passing traffic along the lane

below, so no prying eyes can peer in at this private world. Nowadays, the self-conscious melancholy is unwittingly enhanced by the decay all around: the low box (*Buxus*) hedges are ragged, the seats mossily uninviting, the delicate tracery of ironwork rusty and broken. But it is all here, and the makers' presence is powerfully felt.

Up a broad flowing staircase, adorned by spectacular columns with slender dragons balancing on top, the visitor reaches the next terrace, and the Garden of Joy. Here, Venus emerges from a pond in her shell chariot drawn by two seahorses into a floral parterre. The statue is crude (though the seahorses, with their webbed hoofs, flaring nostrils and twisty reins, are much better) and the parterres are grimly neglected, but the message of bright happiness is clear enough. It would not be difficult to reinstate the former splendour here. The next level, the Garden of the Hours, is a simple gravelled terrace with a sundial surrounded by the signs of the zodiac. The views are cleverly handled: in one direction is the ancient church tower soberly framed in cypresses (*Cupressus*); and, in the other, all is oriental, with palms, obelisks and Japanese planting, including a big

BELOW The terrace vista includes Hercules in his niche screening the townscape of Pallanza beyond, so that it appears as a wood with a few scattered villas. The famous prospect over the lake is deliberately restricted to the top terrace.

Japanese cedar (*Cryptomeria*) and the green spines, white flowers and little oranges of Japanese bitter orange (*Citrus trifoliata*). This latter rises from a naturalistic rock garden, which spreads across the width of the terrace, raised against the retaining wall. It continues into a glasshouse now mysteriously gloomy and largely populated by overgrown *Aspidistra* and the unearthly blue glow of *Begonia* which have naturalized themselves among the rocks. This structure seems to have been one of Sophie's favourite corners of the garden, in which she liked to be photographed among the troglodyte scenery. Below, the visitor begins to see the famous scenes of the lake and mountains beyond, but it is becoming apparent that these are intended to be viewed from the balconies of the house.

At this point a little detour is called for. A short walk leads through a grove of *Camellia*, lovely in their quiet variety, to the *hortus conclusus*, a little shady space of which one side is formed by the north wall of the ancient church. Another side is closed by a length of wall clearly built to echo the medieval fabric. Some of this 'modern' wall has been constructed using ancient techniques, including the herringbone stonework found in Anglo-Saxon churches.

In the middle of this enclosure is a pool in the form of a square overlaid with a circle, symbolizing the earth and heaven interlocked, and four straight lines of stone run out perpendicularly from the sides of the square, suggesting the four rivers of Paradise – water, wine, milk and honey – as represented in Moorish gardens such as the Court of

---

BELOW The groups of conversing aesthetes are long gone now, but the setting remains. The view from the terrace extends across the lake to Laveno at the foot of the Sasso del Ferro.

OPPOSITE Granite half-columns support an arch in a loggia. Beyond, a statue on the terrace contemplates the scene over the Borromean Gulf.

the Lions at the Alhambra. The planting is of course all evergreen, and includes the slender cypress of Italy (*Cupressus sempervirens*) and the Irish yew (*Taxus baccata* 'Fastigiata'). Everything speaks of silence, ancient peace, and the universality of faith.

Back on the main route, the next terrace up keeps perhaps more of its original character than any other in the garden, simply because the surfaces are easily maintained by mowing and clipping, so that everything is still in good order. This is the Garden of Springs, or of Scents – nobody seems sure which. Every visitor should walk across its rectangular lawns, so that their tread can release the delicious perfume of thyme into the air. It is at moments such as these that Sophie and Silvio's continuing presence is felt. The back wall is also covered in perfumed greenery, being decorated

ABOVE The exedra in the Garden of Sighs presents a semicircular wall of alternating gods in niches and panels of delicate mosaic, including fading silhouettes of Silvio and Sophie Della Valle di Casanova.

RIGHT The rather ominous staircase from the top terrace to the Garden of Sighs is framed in yew (*Taxus*) topiary, including obelisks which have become gradually more bloated over the years. At the top is a rosy coat of arms.

in broad pilasters of myrtle. There is genuine evocative originality here overlying the outward simplicity. Four panels of sculpture and mosaic alternate with the panels of myrtle, forming a Latin inscription from Horace's Epodes:

> Fontesque lymphis obstreperunt manantibus
> Somnos quod invitet leves.
> [Where the liquid fountain flows
> Which with its murmurs courts us to repose.]

ABOVE The exedra in the Garden of Sighs is here seen from a pool in the Garden of Memories. From this point, the whole sequence from the exedra to the top of the staircase can be identified, including part of the imaginary 'cascade' of white azaleas (*Rhododendron*) which 'flows' in the spring.

The house, on the top terrace, is not open to the public, unless you want to get married in the one unaltered room. The visitor therefore then crosses the terrace to begin their descent to more gardens. Just as they do so, there is a stone panel set into a decorative wall bearing an Italian inscription which translates as: 'We, Silvio and Sophie, who met here in childhood, made this garden, born of a shared dream of youth and completed as man and wife.'

A little further on another inscription explains that the project was begun in 1887 and finished in 1916. It is worth reflecting that Silvio and Sophie's neighbour was Luigi Cadorna, commander of the Italian army which joined the First World War in 1915.

On the northern side of the Villa San Remigio, facing the industrial town of Intra (once the 'Manchester of

Lombardy'), a long staircase extends down the hill. It is lined on either side by a yew (*Taxus*) hedge cut into topiary, including some now rather overweight-looking obelisks. The flanking slopes are largely planted with white-flowering azaleas (*Rhododendron*), perhaps simply to brighten up this shady slope, but the impression lingers of a silent torrent of water cascading down.

At the foot of the slope is a great semicircular exedra, a retaining wall set alternately with statues in niches and panels of mosaic. This is the Garden of Sighs, with its inscription dated 1902. The mosaics include silhouettes of Silvio and

TOP The standard of maintenance in the Garden of Sadness is barely sufficient. It would be easy enough to regenerate the hedges, but the failure of the stonework revealed by the modern supports is a more serious problem to put right.

OPPOSITE BELOW Spindly roses hang on in the Garden of Joy. Beyond the putto, Venus drives her chariot out of the sea and through a parterre of flowers which just retains enough its former character to trigger the imagination.

ABOVE Sophie Della Valle di Casanova looks out wistfully from among the ferns in one of the sub-terrace conservatories, at the beginning of the twentieth century. Her favourite ornamental-leaved *Begonia* are by her side: they survive *in situ*.

OPPOSITE ABOVE Sophie was often photographed in the gloomy solitude of her conservatories, as though she were a Georgian lady patiently refining the shellwork on her grotto walls.

Sophie facing each other, decorated with delicate ribbons in terracotta. The whole thing was perhaps suggested by the great exedra at the Villa Aldobrandini in Frascati – another garden in dire need of attention.

Beyond this, a broad level lawn with formal ponds and vases comprises the Garden of Memories, with roses everywhere. The terrace looks over Sophie's ample studio at the end of a little avenue, and leads away to the place where the visitor came in. Yet another inscription reminds us that: 'Rosae transeunt, memoria manet.' [Roses fade, but memory remains.]

Silvio died in 1929, but Sophie lived on until 1960 – the wonder of the age. Their daughter, Esther, inherited some of her mother's durability, and became a well-known mountaineer. She eventually left the garden to the local authority. Her own daughter is an occasional modern visitor. The tourist office arranged guided visits to the site until the big storm of August 2012, which smashed steps and balustrades, brought down columns and statues, and uprooted trees, so that public access is, at the time of writing, indefinitely denied. The damage is severe, but not terminal. If the political will is there, wonderful things can be achieved. Some vigorous campaigning by a local friends' group, accompanied by a chorus of international acclaim for the significance of the garden, would be a big help.

Until that happens, the balustrades will crumble, the inscriptions will fade, brambles will steal through the woods, and the Villa San Remigio – a place where taste, sentiment and original thinking come unexpectedly together – will remain just beyond everyone's reach.

LEFT With its pools and vases, lawns and balustrades, the Garden of Memories is deliberately quiet and reflective, as the final episode in the story. A few roses linger on, prompting the intended pleasing melancholy.

VILLA DELLA PORTA
BOZZOLO

The broad valley of the Valcúvia, east of Lake Maggiore, is rather off the beaten track for the tourist, but well worth seeking out by anyone interested in seeing a magnificent, eighteenth-century garden attached to a villa of considerable beauty, all in smiling countryside rising all around to wooded alpine foothills. Despite the best efforts of the Fondo per l'Ambiente Italiano (FAI) – the Italian equivalent of the National Trust – the Villa Della Porta Bozzolo remains one of those Wordsworthian treasures which nature keeps to herself. It is therefore something of a shock to anyone driving along the valley road through the pleasant but unassuming village of Casalzuigno to glance to the north and see what appears to be a sort of green rocket launcher, flanked by pointed cypresses (*Cupressus sempervirens*), shooting up the mountainside. Fortunately, it is easy to examine this phenomenon closer to hand, because there is a convenient car park nearby. Walking up to the property, pretty much the only thing that can be seen from the outside is the view that first catches the attention of passers-by; the rest of Villa Della Porta Bozzolo is screened by tall walls. The visitor looks in though handsome wrought iron gates, clearly intended to allow the envious traveller to see how the great and good live but not actually to join in the fun. The framed view leads the eye across a level space, then up some monumental terraces via a broad staircase, all saved from overbearing pomposity by being built of the local, rather handsome limestone from

nearby Viggiù, right on the Swiss border. At each half-landing the balustrade is adorned with a big lemon (*Citrus × limon*) pot. Then the slope begins. At first, it opens out into a vast octagonal lawn on an even gradient, framed by stone retaining walls, with slender cypresses maintaining a slow but steady architectural rhythm round the outside. At the top of this lawn is a bit more terracing, finishing in a sort of balcony from which some dignitary can be imagined making a speech to a multitude assembled below. They would have to have a voice like a foghorn to make themselves heard. Behind and above this platform, the aforementioned rocket launcher begins its relentless, dead-straight progress up the rest of the valley side, the lining of cypresses, now more closely packed, serving to suggest speed and power up the slope until the whole process ends in the sky.

All this designed magnificence is derived from the idea of the baroque, that cult of personal magnificence which ran through Europe in the seventeenth and early eighteenth centuries. This idea of a central axis of startling length – the longer the better – became fixed in the mind of European landowners in the wake of Louis XIV's Versailles, where, just like here, the envious crowd could peer in through elaborate railings at great men doing distinguished things. At Versailles, though, as at all its other imitators across Europe (and there were many) the eye is stopped by the front door of the palace dead ahead, and only the elite can look beyond it to the continuing central axis through the garden, out into the park and beyond. Here, we expect to see the Villa Bozzolo, but there is nothing there. Those terraces, that octagonal lawn, that steep avenue of cypresses should rise behind it. Given the inflexibility of baroque protocol, this must have been a little unnerving for the gentleman caller of 1720.

OPPOSITE The view downhill from the great octagon looks over the terraces, through the courtyard of honour and, ultimately, up to the peak of the Monte Campo dei Fiori. The villa is on the right, facing the earlier axis.

The answer to the mystery lies in the gradual upward mobility of the family here during the two centuries before this part of the garden was laid out. The house was built for the Della Porta family in the early sixteenth century as a working farm, and the surviving outbuildings show convincing evidence of vineyard and silkworm culture, so that we can readily imagine these slopes covered in the regular patterns of vineyards and mulberry (*Morus*) groves. In the second half of the century, the property was upgraded to the status of a villa – the seat of a gentleman farmer – with one document referring to the house as the *domus magna* [great house]. During the seventeenth century, this social progress continued, and the trappings of success began to appear around the house in the form of polite courtyards and a garden pushing out into the rural setting.

The great leap forward to the present exceptional layout came during the ownership of Gian Angelo III Della Porta, a young man of wealth and ideas who married Isabella Giulini in 1711, at the age of twenty-one. This seems to have been the great moment in the estate's history. Gian Angelo retained the basic structure of the house, with its

TOP A postcard of the early twentieth century shows the view up the terraces looking very much as it does now, with the rhythm punctuated by big pots of lemons (*Citrus × limon*). The family dog made a memorable appearance at that moment.

ABOVE Handsome detailing of carved stone vases, welcoming putti and big pots of lemons decorate a corner of the courtyard of honour.

OPPOSITE The newly reset steps of the terraces look a little bare without their lemon pots. The whole structure is a monumental achievement in ornamental architecture, inlaid with panels of decorative stonework.

square Renaissance courtyard and dog-leg staircase strikingly reminiscent of the Villa Cicogna Mozzoni not so far away, and opened up a new garden in the baroque manner on the other side. A bigger square was levelled out to form the courtyard of honour, a place of state and parade closed by a decorative wall topped with swagger statues of the four seasons variously posturing. A gateway opens in the centre of this wall and leads on to an avenue of trees, now limes (*Tilia*), terminating in an open temple showing a large fresco by Giovan Battista Ronchelli of Apollo and a selection of Muses disporting themselves on the flanks of Mount Parnassus. This orderly sequence, measured to the middling scale of the owner's position in society, looks especially lovely when seen from the ideal viewpoint of the *piano nobile* [first-floor] balcony of the house. A geometric garden is intended to be enjoyed from the *piano nobile*, whence it makes more sense to the ordered mind.

The neat and regular layout at Villa Dela Porta Bozzolo, satisfying all the design requirements of the age, might have been thought complete as it was. Within a few years, however, and perhaps in the 1720s, the spectacular layout visible from the entrance gate was constructed. This runs at a right angle across the very same courtyard in front of the house, using it for the same visual function, but then begins its monumental ascent up the valley side to the top. It is this very defiance of the topography which makes it exceptional. The obvious thing to do is to lay out the long axis in the form of an avenue or a canal along the valley floor, but launching it up the valley side is taking a big idea to an extreme. The only other place I have come across such an idea is at Linderhof, in the Bavarian Alps. There, Ludwig II's gardener Carl von Effner similarly slung the long axis across the valley – in that case up both sides – with magnificent effect, but that was in the nineteenth century, and done for a king noted for his dramatic gestures rather than for a country gentleman in a quiet corner of Lombardy. Perhaps the owner here was unable to extend the earlier axis because he did not control the land beyond it, and so resorted to the present original tactic. He must have known it would bring him either ridicule or glory. Since the documentary record appears to be silent, perhaps no one took much notice – the worst fate of all.

At the same time as all these great works were in progress in the garden, the house at Villa Della Porta Bozzolo received a comprehensive makeover. Its structure remained unaltered, but the interior was turned into a delicate riot, if such a thing is possible, of painted decoration. Every surface – whether walls, ceilings or doors – was covered in rococo frescoes, in something of a rustic hand. All of these survive, and confirm the visitor's impression that the garden theme is important here, and flowers most of all. *Trompe l'oeil* swags are everywhere, and even the shutters are stippled with stylized flowers in pretty spring colours. This is especially the case in the entrance hall, where the mountain breeze blows gently through the open doors along the line of the axis. Upstairs a broad corridor is frescoed with figures from the classical world, twirling in rococo attitudes, conferring a light and happy atmosphere on the house.

The present lovely condition of the house and garden gives little hint of the long years of decline. After the Della Porta line failed in 1814, the estate passed through several owners before coming to rest in the hands of Camillo Bozzolo, senator in the new nation of Italy. It finally passed from his heirs to the FAI in 1989. Since then, the house has returned to life along with its illustrious garden. Most of the present house furnishings have been brought from elsewhere to

BELOW The layout is relieved from monumentality by the overlay of greenery. A simple turf parterre has lemon (*Citrus* × *limon*) pots at its corners in traditional style, and circular flower beds within each panel.

replace the losses of the post-war years, when this estate entered a long decline. In the early years of the FAI rescue, I recall the sound of the portable radio drifting through the house as unseen conservators cleaned the ceiling frescoes on scaffolding above my head.

Events of various kinds now bring the place to life, such as the festival of food and drink, which fills the outbuildings in early autumn. Local families enjoy the place at weekends. A lot of the pleasure in this garden resides in the careful integration of flower plantings into the great geometric layout. Simple circular beds of seasonal flowers enliven the level lawns in the courtyard of honour, and big terracotta lemon (*Citrus × limon*) pots frame this space, leading the eye from it up the great terrace steps, where they are placed at

ABOVE The long shadows of the cypress (*Cupressus sempervirens*) fall across the turf octagon below the pulpit-like viewing platform. The rigour of the baroque soon dissolves into romantic ease in the face of nature's endless variety.

LEFT The earlier axis is best seen from the ideal viewpoint of the balcony on the first floor of the house. The line proceeds through a gate screen surmounted by figures of the seasons, then along an avenue of limes (*Tilia*) to an open temple dedicated to Apollo and the Muses.

intervals along the balustrades in a classical rhythm. Where these steps meet the base of the great octagon lawn, lines of pale blue *Iris* run along the base of low retaining walls to either side, indicating the little sentry-box temples at the ends of the lateral walks. In early spring, the whole space of the sloping octagon lawn is covered in *Crocus*, half a million of which were planted here under the direction of the architect Emilio Trabella in 2003. These are multicoloured and intermingled in the Italian taste.

OPPOSITE Stonework and greenery assemble in rank order viewed from the balcony. A parterre of crushed brick sits at the foot of the terraces.
ABOVE Hercules strangles the Hydra at the foot of the octagon, as stately cypresses (*Cupressus sempervirens*) lead the eye up the slope to the final narrow ascent.
OVERLEAF The triumphal rhythms of the descending axis of honour are trumpeted by the flanking statues and adorned by the lemon (*Citrus × limon*) pots, leading the eye out into open country. The house, which should be the focal point, is here a polite onlooker.

Continuing round the edge of the octagon, the regularly spaced cypresses (*Cupressus*), which were in a poor and uneven state in the 1990s, have all been replanted and are looking well. It is rather optimistic to expect such sun-worshippers to flourish in this northern latitude, so the time may come when the exercise will have to be repeated. On reaching the base of the final steep slope, again lined with a cypress avenue, the visitor realizes that, although the slope looks daunting from the house, closer examination reveals a zigzag ramp ascending to the top in a perfectly reasonable pattern of ascent. On a Sunday afternoon, the steady progress of individuals working their way up and down at different levels has a vaguely operatic quality. At the top, the climber is met with a blank wall, but the return view makes all the effort worthwhile. The eye skims back down the narrow sloping avenue, out over the broad lawn of the octagon, across the courtyard of honour, out through the iron-grille gate and straight down the lane to the main road. Just across it, the visual progress is momentarily halted by a

modern shop (groan), but the imagination soon brushes it aside and the straight line continues up the wooded hill on the other side of the valley and up to the peak of the Monte Campo dei Fiore, the charmingly named Mountain of the Field of Flowers. At first, it seems unsatisfactory that this peak is not aligned on the axis, but it should be remembered that to the baroque mind that would be inappropriate. The mountain is an unaltered remnant of divine Creation, whereas the garden is a modern work of his servant, and for the peak to be included in the geometry of the layout might seem a stretch too far for vaunting man. The same phenomenon can be witnessed in the garden at Powerscourt in Co. Wicklow, in Ireland, where the Sugarloaf rises up beyond the garden in much the same way, but remains similarly somewhat left of centre. There are limits to human ambition.

It would be easy to imagine that these two worlds – the artificial and the natural – should be kept strictly apart in a garden such as this, where man's control over nature is demonstrated so comprehensively. But the present owners have given these matters careful thought, and come up with an ingenious compromise. Where the long steep avenue shoots up the hill on its final journey, the native flora is allowed to bloom freely, at least in spring. The underlying rock being limestone, and fertilizers and herbicides never being used, the result is a wonderfully rich and diverse botanist's delight.

In mid-spring, the foot of the avenue, for those who cannot face the long walk, overflows with soapwort (*Saponaria*) and every kind of trefoil (*Trifolium*), and for those with a keen eye there are plenty of early orchids sprouting here and there alongside the path. Of course, the vegetation has to be cut down periodically to prevent the whole thing reverting to woodland.

Autumn at the Villa Della Porta Bozzolo also has its pleasures, such as an abundance of centaury (*Centaurium*). Half the fun for the visitor is the pleasure taken both by

BELOW Some of the decorative stonework, such as these urn finials, has had to be remade in modern times. Likewise, the noble cypresses (*Cupressus sempervirens*) lining the octagon have been replanted in the past twenty years.

those who recognize these beauties and those who do not, for whom the scene is merely a Shakespearian flowery bank. This is a model of how a historic garden should be managed in modern times.

There will always be those who, with reason, look back wistfully to a time when this garden was a private pleasure ground viewed from a house filled with the intimate atmosphere which can only exist in a family home. But when the alternative is gradual ruin and loss, the best way forward

must be that balance of historical understanding, skilled craftsmanship and intelligent management which adds up to good conservation practice. We should be grateful that the Villa Della Porta Bozzolo, on this secluded hillside, has survived at all. This exceptional place is so well presented that it should be on the itinerary of every enlightened visitor to the Italian Lakes.

ABOVE LEFT In a vision of harmony, the eye is led out from the villa along the avenue, and the eighteenth-century decoration defers to the garden. Flowers are included at every turn, and the pale sky of the north floats on the ceiling.

ABOVE RIGHT In the reverse view from the parterre, we can see the entertaining frescoed panels on the external walls. The eye is drawn straight through the house and across an inner court to another fresco closing the vista.

VILLA CICOGNA
MOZZONI

One day in the late 1950s, the young Eleonore Paar, an employee of the Thomas Cook travel agency in Lugano, went out for her usual weekend cycling trip in the countryside. On these jaunts she enjoyed visiting old country houses and their gardens, and on that day she found herself in the village of Bisúschio, a few kilometres north of Varese, where she knew that there was a very interesting example tucked away round a corner. She rode into the courtyard, knocked at the door and asked if she could have a look round. The dowager countess was so surprised that this intrepid young woman had come all that way on her bicycle that she invited her to join the family for lunch. At the lunch table was, among others, her son. Everyone who ever met the Contessa Cicogna Mozzoni, as Eleonore Paar became, will remember her exceptional gifts as a guide to her family home. Each performance was a little different, but always with that unique combination of comprehensive knowledge and personal warmth. She was at all times perfectly correct and disarmingly humorous. Once in my earshot a visitor remarked that the grass could do with cutting. 'Don't be so bourgeois' came the reply, with a wave of the hand, and we marched on to discuss more important matters in one of the seven languages at her fluent command. She is gone now, but her son, Jacopo Cicogna Mozzoni, continues the tradition and is himself now the personification of this place, with its special atmosphere. It is rare enough to find a private country estate in Italy intact with its

ancestral set piece of house and garden looking as it did in photographs of a century ago and entirely untouched by the dead hand of the restorer. How much rarer to find an owner perfectly in sympathy with all this historical significance, and willing to show cultural pilgrims all over the place, explain how it all fits together, and recall how the family have lived and used the place down the ages and into modern times. The villa and its garden are an exceptional survival of the design ideas of the mid-sixteenth century, when the Italian Renaissance was beginning to wander off into that more freely decorative phase called Mannerism. The story began in 1476, when the all-powerful duke of Milan, Galeazzo Maria Sforza, was entertained to a bear-hunt at the Mozzoni family's hunting lodge. At some point in the proceedings, the duke got into difficulty with a bear, whereupon Agostino Mozzoni's dog leapt at the great beast's throat and managed to hold things up until order was restored. The heroic dog's bronze image lies on a special red velvet cushion in the best room in the house to this day. Understandably, the duke was obliged for this timely intervention, and privileges were showered on the Mozzoni family, leading to the conversion, over the next century, of the hunting lodge into the villa and garden we see today.

The hunting lodge, at the front of the courtyard, now forms the entrance range, while the remainder of the villa is on two further sides of the square. There is always a good deal of doubt as to whether this courtyard is part of the house or the garden, since all around are frescoed walls and, under the arcaded loggia, a frescoed ceiling, with the garden comprising the fourth side of the square. The paintings exposed to the sun are faded and chalky, but still reveal damsels leaning out

OPPOSITE A trinkling fountain in the parterre at the Villa Cicogna Mozzoni. Beyond it lies the entrance court, with the arcade along one side. The frescoes have been gradually fading for 450 years.

of imaginary windows to see if the huntsmen have returned from the woods, and there is also a painted horizon which joins the real one framed in the entrance arch. The ceiling, however, is as brilliant as when it was new, and shows, among other things, the family arms and a selection of relevant deities, displayed along a painted garden pergola. Some of these frescoes are the work of the Campi brothers of Cremona, pupils of the great proto-baroque architect Giulio Romano. Anyone who begins to take a lively interest in these

ABOVE Two rectangular pools on one side of the garden balance the hedges, lawns and flowers on the other. The entrance court and the garden are conceived as a unit: the bay laurel (*Laurus nobilis*) hedge continues the line of the hunting lodge wing.

RIGHT The purpose of moving water in a garden is to entertain and surprise. Here, a putto gets a refreshing shower from a dolphin's mouth, while a deity looks soberly on from a niche in a tufa dressed retaining wall.

things in the courtyard will be completely overwhelmed by those within the villa itself.

On the open side of this entrance court is the *giardino grande*, a matching square of geometric planting and ponds, framed by a tall hedge and retaining walls, with the steep hill rising behind. It is immediately obvious what a feat of engineering it must have been to cut these levels out of the bank and shore them all up. The proximity of this cultivated scene and the dramatic countryside emphasizes the idea of the villa as a place to escape from the business of the town and get back in touch with nature. A greater contrast with the centre of Milan is hard to conceive.

It would be a mistake, however, to think that cultural sophistication was left behind in the big city. The whole integrated scheme of house and garden here at Villa Cicogna Mozzoni is worked out in marvellous detail. Anyone wanting to understand the garden should go round the house and spot how the different levels and components marry together in a way that is both meticulous and an unfolding revelation.

It is the small details which register at first: the use of the same three stone colours – pink, grey and black – to pave the half-landing of the staircase and to cover the gravel walks of the garden; the same pattern of balustrade on the staircase, on the adjoining fresco and framing the garden ponds; the painted border of garden vegetables around the family portraits in the *salone*; and the appearance of Roman deities engaged in rustic chivalry at every turn. All these patterns and themes are characteristic of the Italian garden of the sixteenth century, and they are the very foundation on which the garden history of the world rests. These are big ideas, but here they gradually unfold before the observant visitor who can hardly do other than smile at every turn; the story proceeds as tellingly now as it did then.

BELOW House and garden merge seamlessly in the arcaded loggia. Doorways lead the eye into the parterre, while a sixteenth-century fresco depicts the all-important bear hunt which made the family's name.

Standing in the courtyard garden, the ingenious unity of the scheme gradually becomes apparent. On one side of the square is a simple geometry of turf, box and flower beds: a parterre. On the other side is a pair of rectangular ponds, neatly dividing the whole space into land on one side and water on the other. The enclosing boundary is the same height on three sides. On one side, it is a stone retaining wall, and there is a bay laurel (*Laurus nobilis*) hedge opposite it – a 'dead' wall and a living one. On closer examination, the stone wall is seen to be faced with tufa from the inside of limestone caves, including ancient sponges and stalactites, so that this ancient fossilized life contrasts with the modern living tissue of the hedge. Cut into the face of the tufa wall are niches, with the figure of Hercules in the central one, often an image cultivated by villa owners who wished to associate themselves with the idea of the half-man, half-god who, confronted with apparently impossible tasks, knocked them off with ease.

Here and there in the gravel, traces can be seen of the system of *giochi d'acqua* [water games], which once spouted up when a tap was turned by an unseen hand to soak the unwary.

Jacopo Cicogna Mozzoni remembers firing up the system on (in)appropriate occasions as a boy, to the mortification of his father. One day, it will work again, and on that occasion the visitor should remember, as with such systems in other gardens, that it pays to walk along the middle of the path under the arch of water, and that those who flee to the edge get the full benefit of a refreshing shower on a sunny day. After walking through the little grotto – a place for sitting in cool shade in the heat of summer – the visitor climbs up to the height of the framing wall, which brings them to a long terrace on the same level as the best rooms in the house on the *piano nobile*. From here, they can look down on the neat pattern of the parterre and ponds, with the mountains rising behind.

A walk along the terrace, where lemon (*Citrus* × *limon*) pots alternate with big specimens of *Osmanthus fragrans*, whose

---

ABOVE The 'dead' wall of the parterre is a substantial retaining structure. It is dressed with tufa, limestone from the interior of caves, including some stalactites and stalagmites. The central niche features Hercules dispatching the Nemean lion.

memorable scent drifts on the air in the autumn, brings the visitor to the unexpected pleasure of the water staircase flowing down the steep hill. As at the famous Villa Lante at Bagnaia and at Caprarola, the silent stream glitters down its narrow course flanked by steps either side leading to the open temple at the top. It will reward the visitor to arrive at this view as the makers intended, by emerging from the glazed doors of the *salone*, which cleverly align an enfilade of rooms with the cascade, reminding us of the unity of ideas which pervaded the sixteenth-century designer's mind. At the far end of this terrace, a stone staircase turns up the slope and leads into the woods above. This powerful contrast between the controlling hand of man and the dark forces of nature reflects, knowingly, the opening lines of Dante's *Inferno*, where the hero finds, midway on his journey through life, that he comes to himself in a dark wood, where the straight road is lost.

The climb to the top is not for everyone, but there a different world opens up, with a slight winding watercourse bringing the supply to the head of the water staircase, while the

land falls away on the other side into an undulating park of big trees in the English style. Walking down through it, the visitor soon comes to a range of glasshouses and a wall of flowers for cutting, before returning to the terrace viewpoint seen before.

Many foreign visitors over the years have been pleasantly surprised to find such a place as the Villa Cicogna Mozzoni on the northern edge of Lombardy, near the Swiss border, with mountains and woods all around. Edwardian travellers were more used to looking for such places in the countryside around Florence, so it must have been rather a treat to find this treasure conveniently near to the watering holes of the northern lakes. Some of those who were prepared to travel over hill and dale recorded their names in the guest book in the years before the First World War, when Count Gian

BELOW The lawns to the north of the house look towards Lake Lugano. A constant theme in both house and garden is the balustrading – always the same pattern, whether in stone or painted on the wall.

Pietro Cicogna Mozzoni humoured callers by letting them look over the place. Some of them signed their names in the guest book. Although Edith Wharton, who enthused over the garden in *Italian Villas and their Gardens*, did not record her presence here, it was noted by Maxfield Parrish, who famously illustrated Wharton's book (much to her disgust, and greatly to its commercial advantage), when he came with his wife on 20 May 1903.

The following year, perhaps with the new book in the glove compartment, Sir George Sitwell, gathering evidence for his own book *On the Making of Gardens*, turned up with his travelling companion, the garden designer Francis Inigo Thomas. Mary Berenson came the following day, and made a second visit later in the year, no doubt while her husband Bernard, the great art historian of the age, was peering at old masters in Lombard convents. A few years later, the dauntless mountaineer and photographer Mrs Aubrey Le

ABOVE Jacopo Cicogna Mozzoni is the present family member responsible for the conservation and presentation of the house and garden. Like others before him, he does it all with knowledge, understanding, wit and warmth.

Blond published her own book *The Old Gardens of Italy: How to Visit Them*, and included a picture of the courtyard garden at the Villa Cicogna Mozzoni, which she described as 'the most enchanting little sunk *giardino segreto* I have ever seen'. The sentiment might be slightly exaggerated, since it is neither a *giardino segreto* nor sunk, but only a stony-hearted visitor would be unmoved by this place.

Among the many pleasures here, not the least is its sense of peaceful seclusion. Walking to the entrance accompanied by the attention of neighbouring dogs and cats and the clanging of church bells, it is easy to imagine that commercial concerns have no place here. But if this garden, and others like it, are to remain well cared for and open to the public, more visitors must come. If the Villa Cicogna Mozzoni stood on the shore of either of the big lakes, it would be perpetually overrun by admiring crowds. Its position between the two, however, and a little off the beaten track, means that only the devotees make it here. For those in search of the genuine article, looking for something to add to their list of the great gardens of Italy, this is the place.

OPPOSITE Troublesome golden-haired little boys clamber about on the imaginary pergola depicted on the frescoed ceiling of the loggia. They are naturally attracted by the lemons (*Citrus × limon*), the grapes (*Vitis*) and the peacock.

BELOW Looking from the parterre to the villa, the steeply rising ground behind the house is striking. It was a considerable feat of sixteenth-century engineering to carve out this plot of level ground.

VILLA PALLAVICINO

The Villa Pallavicino, on the southern outskirts of the pleasant lakeside town of Stresa, is one of the minor attractions of Lake Maggiore. It cannot compete with the great and famous names nearby, and there is inevitably doubt in the prospective visitor's mind as to whether they really want to make a special excursion to a garden which sells itself as a wildlife park. However, there is no need to worry. It is a worthy destination in its own right. By all means join the throng on the terraces of justly famous Isola Bella, but, if there is time, the Villa Pallavicino has much to offer the lover of plants, atmosphere and scenery. The villa stands on the site of a plot bought by Ruggiero Bonghi in 1855. Bonghi was a significant player in Italy's eventually successful struggle for unification in the nineteenth century, which meant that his fortunes rose and fell according to the political situation. He became a member of the nation's first parliamentary assembly, and later education minister, and was famed for his caustic speeches. In old age, Bonghi had the satisfaction of walking into restaurants to general applause and nods of acknowledgment.

In 1862, Bonghi's little house was bought by the Marchese Pallavicino, who promptly set about buying adjacent plots along the shore and up the mountainside, to form the present magnificent site affording sensational views across Lake Maggiore. A villa was built in a key position to feast on that view, and an elaborate layout was created in the manner of the English landscape garden – the dominant style in Italy at the time. In *Italian Villas and their Gardens,* Edith Wharton was dubious about such gardens, believing them to be alien to the Italian tradition, and others have followed her line since, yet this is unfair. They deserve to take their place in the long evolution of styles, and this is a worthy example – and, in parts, among the best.

The layout of the grounds is ingenious, and aimed at the man of feeling. A broad carriage drive rises gradually from the road by the shore, briefly looking out over the lake before plunging into scenery of a quite different character. All around is evidence of a conflict between two approaches to garden creation, with one constantly making dents in the other before steadily being overwhelmed by superior forces. Spindly borders of bulbs, *Dahlia* and *Hydrangea* edge the drive, and a big effort is made on one corner with the words Villa Pallavicino in dwarf topiary, but all this superficial knick-knackery is no match for the rocks, moss and ferns of the rugged mountain flank, which looms above. Everywhere nature has enhanced the work of the gardeners by rearranging seeds and spores so they develop into more convincing patterns. The rustic retaining walls, themselves surely hewn from the same ground to form the drives and levels, sprout the descendants of the very plants introduced by previous generations of gardeners, but now they are self-sustaining, watered by the alpine rivulet rather than the hosepipe. Just beyond the would-be pomp of the aforementioned flower bed is a glorious bank of royal fern (*Osmunda regalis*), looking as happy as can be sticking out of the rocky wall where the seeping flush of mineral-laden water keeps its roots permanently supplied with just the kind of sodden organic matter it loves.

OPPOSITE The Villa Pallavicino, a handsome, mid-nineteenth-century house superbly positioned a short distance south of Stresa, commands the bay from its woods and flower gardens.

On the bank above this vision of the forest, other plants have grown similarly. *Hosta* and ivies (*Hedera*), solomon's seal (*Polygonatum*) and violets have all shuffled themselves around over a century and a half to form the kind of vision of a woodland garden which appeared in William Robinson's speculative book *The Wild Garden* when the garden at Villa Pallavicino was still young. Many a Victorian visitor must have been instantly reminded of the beloved lakes of Killarney, in Ireland – one of the great destinations for those who suffered from pteridomania, the 'fern fever' which swept 1870s society. Above these interesting scenes, the big trees rise, providing the necessary deep but deciduous shade, with a mixed shrub storey intermingled, including many naturalized *Rhododendron* and *Camellia*.

All this is a little unnerving to many visitors of today, who have come in search of sunshine and bright flower beds, but all that is to come later on at Villa Pallavicino. For now, we should immerse ourselves in the drama of the mountain and the flood.

A little further up the drive, another theme in this garden is encountered – that of architectural variety. The Marchese

Pallavicino's architect was correct in wanting to leave his client's villa unencumbered by outworks such as stables and workshops, so he came up with the clever idea of disguising these necessary structures as ornamental buildings strategically located at intervals throughout the grounds, each in its own setting. The first of these on the route is the former stable block, thinly disguised as a rough-rendered Gothick building, perhaps an ancient wayside inn – a happy notion since it now houses a rudimentary café and loo. A little beyond this rustic pavilion, the impression grows that the visitor is entering the setting for one of Grimm's fairy tales. The trees grow even larger, the rush of water is heard, and a tight bend on the path leads to a bridge and a substantial waterfall. This is the high point of the woodland experience at the Villa Pallavicino, and it surely represents the spirit of Romanticism, which is to say the veneration of the power of

ABOVE The modern flower garden, on the site of the former kitchen garden, is a dazzling display of bedding and roses each summer. The nineteenth century glasshouses survive intact, though there is no public access.

the natural world. The cascade, sliding down the rock face like a grey mare's tail, rushes under the bridge, surrounded by green ferns and shrubs, while huge trees tower overhead. The spirits of Wordsworth and Beethoven are here; these are familiar ideas in the UK and Germany but seldom so openly celebrated in Italy, where Dante taught us to fear leaving the straight and narrow for the dangers of the dark forest.

At this point something quite unexpected often breaks through the music of the woodland stream – an exotic bird call. At first, no one can quite place it, except to be sure it is not a European bird. Has the visitor arrived at the entrance to the Lost World? But then comes the realization that in 1952 the marchesa decided to open the grounds to the visiting public, and, like the Marquess of Bath, realized that she would draw the crowds by filling her grounds with foreign wildlife. There are no lions in these woods, but that piercing bird cry was a macaw, whose cage sits next to the café further up. Along the upward route from now on, enclosures appear here and there, populated by desultory emus, storks, deer and what have you. More interesting from the reader's point of view is the approaching house, from which the visitor is kept at a respectful distance. The drive then bends upwards

again, past a group of particularly magnificent tulip trees (*Liriodendron tulipifera*), so huge and prosperous that they look as if they have been here for hundreds of years, though they are surely the same age as the villa.

Further up again, the woodland atmosphere becomes noticeably less dense, and the drive is lined with *Camellia* of many kinds, including autumn-flowering *C. sasanqua*. The light level continues to rise until the visitor suddenly breaks out into the open in a broad swathe of lawn sweeping down to the lake, with the house splendidly framed in the middle. A vast Atlas cedar (*Cedrus atlantica*) revels in this spot, its great spreading crown reaching right down to the lawn all around. Beyond the regular block of the house with its arcaded rhythm of windows, the epic view extends across the lake to the east. It is an impressive composition, made by someone who keenly understood the site and had studied its potential.

BELOW A great cedar (*Cedrus atlantica*) dominates the broad sweep of lawn, which reveals the villa at its foot. Pallanza and the Castagnola promontory form the foreground of the view across the lake.

Soon the visitor arrives at the pleasure centre of the grounds. The long trek up through the woods and waters is a complete contrast with the pleasure grounds which now break on the eye. Straight ahead is the original flower garden, rather clumsily divided between a big rectangular pool with fountains and a circuit walk with moderate architectural decorations. There are dense plantings of ornamental shrubs everywhere, with plenty of show but not much organization. Nonetheless, there is much to enjoy: lovely big *Hydrangea paniculata*, *Caesalpinia* and *Lantana*, which fills Europeans with joy and Australians with horror. There are some very handsome specimen trees on the lawns, especially the big persimmon (*Diospyros kaki*). All around are the minor pleasures of the wildlife park: a black swan cruising between the fountains; a pair of flamingoes in a shallow pond; a ring-tailed coati in an elegant pavilion and the intermittent squawk of those macaws.

The final set piece in this artificial Eden is the former kitchen garden, given away by its level surface laid out as a rectangle with a grid of walks centred on a pool with a twirling putto. There is a handsome range of mid-nineteenth-century glasshouses at one end, the middle section of which is curvilinear. This once-productive layout is now transformed into a rose garden, in which many climbers are trained on arches around the perimeter. It is interesting to see that the rose shoots are tied to the structure with knotted lengths of willow (*Salix*). The intervening beds are a riot of seasonal bedding in a heady brew of colours, in which the unnerving combination of rich yellow and bright pink sears itself into the tissues of the brain. Those who were wondering, back in the forest gloom, whether they would ever get to see any flowers, certainly get their money's worth here. It is all very splendid, and decently maintained, in a way which for once addresses itself to the preferences of the local population. What this garden lacks in refinement it more than makes up for in the marvellous way the landform has been adapted, rather than subjugated, and in the special character of the groves of ornamental woodland which have achieved a grandeur and freedom only possible where nature responds to the designer's proposals.

RIGHT The former kitchen garden walks now form a regular plan for the present crowd-pleasing display of seasonal bedding and roses, centred on the former dipping pond with its putto. Some of the roses are trained on arches around the perimeter.

ALPINIA

Alpinia is a rock garden perched on the mountainside above Stresa, on the western shore of Lake Maggiore. There are various ways to approach it, but the best is via the *funivia* [cable car]. This runs up from the shore at Carciano, where there is a convenient landing stage for the public boat service, towards its final destination on top of Monte Mottarone. The *funivia* takes the visitor to the stop at Alpino, some 800 metres/2,625 feet above sea level. As the *funivia* glides up the bank, there are wonderful perspectives on the scenery immediately below. Villages come and go, but the chief pleasure is looking down on the crowns of big trees and through them to the woodland scenery all around. Soon the *funivia* reaches the stop for Alpinia, and a short walk along a forest track brings the visitor to the garden entrance. By this time, all traces of lakeshore hotel culture are quite forgotten, and the visitor is ready to engage with the world of the knapsack and the walking boot in the fresh mountain air.

Alpinia was founded in 1934 by a group of local enthusiasts keen to make a rock garden for alpine plants in a more appropriate setting than the lakeside town far below. One of the main proponents was Igino Ambrosini, who was also behind the umbrella museum in nearby Gignese. In a fit of misplaced period zeal, they named the new project Duxia, a latinized form of Mussolini's fancy title of the Duce. After the Second World War, this name was quietly replaced by the current one.

A keeper's lodge was built near the entrance to Alpinia, and a network of paths laid out among and between rockwork beds on a large scale. These disappear out of sight round bends, over hills, down slopes and skirting groves of trees. Most of the site was kept clear of woodland in order to afford the alpine species their necessary uninterrupted light and free flow of fresh air. A simple viewing pavilion was constructed to command the view over the lake below. The layout gradually expanded with the passage of time to include a marsh and a circuit walk around the big slope of the valley side.

Experts and specialists, including the distinguished Henri Correvon, conferred as to the nature of the collection, how to assemble it, how to display it and how to manage it from the horticultural point of view and in terms of public access arrangements. Everything was kept plain and simple, so that the plantsman could walk round and receive pleasure and instruction from the collection without being troubled by commercial intrusions. Then, as now, this was to be a place for quiet appreciation of improved nature in an upland setting. Collections were donated, carefully arranged in informal beds among rocks brought from nearby and placed in the right stratification, and the plants accurately labelled. Today, the best time to visit is – as always with alpine plantings – in the spring months. The garden opens at some point in mid-spring, depending on snow conditions. The visitor numbers are pleasantly small, and they are quite likely to be outnumbered by the gardeners working diligently in the beds. Once I walked in and was greeted in silence by the keeper at his cottage door, indicating through universal sign language that his baby daughter was still asleep and that payment could be made on the way out. It is that sort of place.

The walks through the beds proceed gradually away from the lodge, rising informally through the terraced beds towards the pavilion. This is strategically placed to command a monumental view over Lake Maggiore from the west, with the famous islands of Isola Bella, Isola dei Pescatori and Isola Madre magnificently central and the Castagnola peninsula at Pallanza extending behind. At least, I believe this to be the case; on all my visits over the years, misty conditions on the lake have meant that the actual components of the view have been subject to a degree of educated guesswork. Let this caveat not put off anyone coming up here, as there are so many sunny days during the year.

At all points along the walk the scenery changes. Here is a mound through whose surface the natural rock breaks forth. There is a little grove of trees, typically birches (*Betula*) and pines, fringed with bilberries (*Vaccinium*), which form the native ground cover. Under one of these groves is a lovely little moss garden, silvery green and formed of gentle mounds. The track falls away and the visitor enters a shady marsh crossed by a boardwalk, beyond which a long outer circuit wanders away down the slope, eventually to return to the entrance.

The main interest for the enthusiast resides in the beds near the entrance to Alpinia. These are distinctive examples of raised island beds for improved drainage, which is very necessary as the rainfall here is rather too high for many alpine plants. The beds are irregularly shaped and set out on a rough lawn, which must be tricky to mow. The wall of each bed is formed of rough-hewn rock stood on edge, and it is easy to see that the outline must have been largely determined by the available stone, so that there is a heroically makeshift quality to the whole layout. This framework was then filled with layers of rock infill and shingle, gradually building up with greater soil content towards the surface. As this was approached, further rocks set aside for the purpose were introduced, so that the finished appearance reveals their iceberg-like faces, with a topdressing of grit covering the remaining surface between the plants.

The plants themselves are the usual combination of predominantly low-growing shrubs with an admixture of herbaceous perennials. Preference is given to those plants that prefer the natural conditions here – acid soils over granite. The rugged retaining wall along the rising walk is full of heathers (*Calluna*), *Rhododendron* and the native gentians, with a backing of ornamental conifers, some of which are beginning to get overlarge.

BELOW There is no end of pleasure and fascination in gazing out over Lake Maggiore from this considerable height on the flank of Monte Mottarone.

The choicer specimens in some of the beds are grown in an alkaline medium, although of course this will always be something of a gradually losing battle as natural site conditions assert themselves over time. Here is the world of saxifrages, *Sedum*, *Anemone* and dwarf willows (*Salix*), punctuated by the larger meadow rues (*Thalictrum*) and those native ferns which delight in inserting themselves into the rock crevices. There are now significant collections of *Artemisia*, *Campanula*, *Centaurea*, *Dianthus* and *Silene*; given that most of these are native to calcareous soils, the quality of the work here is apparent. The standard of maintenance is universally first class. I can think of nowhere better to spend an enjoyable spring morning out in the fresh air among

fellow enthusiasts quietly rubbing their chins as they debate the accuracy of this label or the position of that *Lewisia*, and then finish by admiring the knockout view over the famous islands in the lake far below. I hope to make them out myself one day.

ABOVE The simple keeper's lodge at the entrance overflows with cheerful window boxes. A sign indicates the way through the raised beds. Fuss here is kept to a minimum: this is a place for the enthusiast.

BOTANIC GARDEN OF THE BRISSAGO ISLANDS

And now for an excursion into Switzerland. At all points in this region of Italy, Switzerland looms on the horizon, its towering peaks ever visible but somehow never quite within reach. The Swiss border is in fact a short run from most places on Lake Como, and the northern end of Lake Maggiore is indeed in Switzerland. The city of Locarno sits on the north-west shore of the lake. The same dialect of Italian is spoken either side of the border. For the garden visitor to Lake Maggiore, the big attraction at the Swiss end is the botanic garden on the larger of the two islands of Brissago. The lake boat service calls in at the little town of Brissago on the mainland. There is little to interest the traveller here unless they are a fan of Ruggero Leoncavallo, the composer of *Pagliacci*, whose summer home stood in Brissago until some philistines demolished it some years ago. In compensation, there is now a charming museum full of touching memorabilia, including CDs of his thirty-nine other operas, which I challenge the reader to list. Local ferries run at intervals from Brissago, and also from nearby Porto Ronco, to the islands. The journey is longer than might be expected on these lakes, as the islands are a good kilometre from the shore. This is a good thing in my opinion, as it gives the mind time to change gear and get into island mode.

On the approach, the visitor can see that both islands are well wooded, of a sufficient size to be worth inhabiting, at least on an extended-holiday basis, and romantically situated. They look irresistible from the shore, and the more so the nearer the visitor gets. The characters in Arthur Ransome's *Swallows and Amazons* would have spent a lot of time mucking about here.

As the boat glides towards the islands, it is evident that one of them – unsurprisingly called the Isola Grande – is much larger than the other. Isola Grande is comprehensively set out as a botanic garden with many visitors in mind, with all the facilities necessary for such an enterprise. Its smaller counterpart is left pretty much to itself. It is also part of the botanic garden, but it is devoted to the natural evolution of its existing flora, and accordingly makes no provision for tourism. The two islands are quite close together, so that it is a surprise to see the substantial ferry sail between them. The botanic garden here is a relatively modern affair, established in 1950 after a long period of private ownership. The two previous occupants had spent a lot of time, effort and money creating their island paradise, and what is seen today is adapted from their layouts, so that the visitor can readily detect three phases of development. The first phase was full of drama and mystery and ended in desperate misery, like a cheap Victorian novel. The second phase put right the practical deficiencies, made a handsome new overlay and laid the foundations for the current layout. The phase – the modern regime – is a model of how to make a tiny garden in the middle of a subalpine lake into an ideal

destination for both plant-lover and traveller in search of scenic beauty followed by an excellent lunch. The whole place makes a marvellous third island garden to compare with Isola Bella and Isola Madre – the more famous ones further south.

There is a medieval and monastic history of the Brissago islands, which is beyond the scope of this book. Our story begins with the acquisition of the island in 1885 by a woman generally referred to as Baroness St Leger. Her story is an improbable one. She seems to have been born Antoinette Bayer in Russia in 1856. There were persistent rumours throughout her life that she was a daughter of Tsar Alexander II. There are several alternative versions of the story. By the time she arrived on the Brissago islands, she was already on to her third husband, an Irishman called Richard Fleming. Quite how the 'baroness' title became attached is not entirely clear to me, or apparently to anyone else. Certainly the wife remains known by it to this day, whereas Richard Fleming seems to have remained just that. Discuss.

The garden on Isola Grande certainly had its origin during this period, at least between its purchase in 1885 and Fleming's departure, apparently demoralized, in 1897. The horticultural enthusiasm seems initially to have been his. Fleming left behind a substantial four-square house and a garden of winding walks around the island, of which perhaps the larger trees, including the specimen palms, on the lawns may be the survivors. 'Baroness' St Leger stayed until 1927, and for some years she continued to develop the planting schemes. A great debt of gratitude is therefore owed for what remains today. Certainly, the planting was in good order when an article appeared in 1912 in the Royal Horticultural Society's *Journal*; it was entitled 'The vegetation of the island of St Leger in Lago Maggiore'. By this time – in the way of

ABOVE A corner of the elegant villa peers through the trees over the swimming-pool enclosure. The lake shore is near enough to form a romantic backdrop, but far enough away to afford the sybaritic seclusion that Max Emden favoured.

such things – the St Leger (pronounced Sellenger) soubriquet had become attached to the island itself, though this was not to last. The article mentioned: 'the huge leaves of *Musa basjoo*', now enjoying a revived popularity as a banana capable of being grown outdoors in Europe; 'immense *Agave* of all species'; '*Hydrangea* in huge clumps'; and, among other things, 'a very artistic, though small, piece of rockery'. This all sounds rather like what is expected on Isola Madre. It is interesting that the author seems to have delivered the paper to the society herself, and perhaps less surprising that she styled herself not a Baroness but Madame Tzikos de St Leger. This latest version of her ever-changing name seems to reflect her fourth marriage, to an Albanian aristocrat called Perikles Tzikos.

In time, the fairy-tale world of Antoinette of the many names and titles disappeared like a puff of smoke. There are stories of speculations in railways, in trams, even in drilling for oil in Romania of all places. These produced less than no income, and things soon went from bad to worse.

BELOW The two Brissago islands are clearly visible on the approach from the lake. The smaller island is managed as a wildlife haven. The botanic garden is on the larger island, with its landing stage and little forest of cultivated trees. The crags rear behind.

Antoinette, alone and in penury, was obliged to sell up. The buyer was Max Emden, a wealthy German entrepreneur, who bought the islands in 1927 and installed Antoinette in a little place on the mainland.

Emden wasted no time in demolishing the existing house and replacing it with the present handsome villa, a neoclassical block saved from looking too much like a hotel by the groups of statues rising from the centre of its roof balustrade. It is ideally placed, raised up sufficiently to command the scene without intruding too much on the natural beauty around it. Emden seems to have done an excellent job all round, stopping the financial rot and bringing the standard of maintenance up to scratch. By his time, the groves of palms and bananas were looking magnificently mature. Down the long lens of history, his may prove to have been the vital tenure, enabling the bright future of what is now visible.

The island, with all its impedimenta, was acquired from Emden's heirs in 1949, by a consortium of local authorities and societies. They wasted no time in establishing it as the Botanic Garden of the (Swiss) Canton Ticino, which has turned out to be a very good idea indeed. Over the years the administrators have found the happy medium: how to attract crowds to see a botanic garden, thus giving it the necessary

specimen trees, and the much expanded 'very artistic, though small, piece of rockery' are still here, and form key components of the many walks. The different parts of Isola Grande are marked out as zones for the cultivation of plants from different regions of the world, with everything correctly and informatively labelled, as it should be in a botanic garden. The lake-dominated conditions readily accommodate species from a wide range of climates and both hemispheres. There is, for example, an interesting collection of *Banksia* (from Australia) and their distant but obvious relations the *Protea* (of South Africa), where the enthusiast can for once see both types growing reasonably contentedly cheek by jowl in a garden setting. Along the rustic pergola, formed simply of blocks of granite set on end, many climbers flourish. Most of them are fairly predictable, but here is lovely *Lapageria* – that vision of smoky crimson – looking perfectly content out of doors against an alpine backdrop.

Everywhere there is variety and excellence. There are shady walks with ferns, broad avenues lined with ornamental shrubs, and a lovely little set piece of a 1930s swimming pool complete with elegant bronze nude female statue in a charming attitude. Behind her is a framed opening in the curtain wall revealing a view of lake and mountains, which the West German Chancellor Konrad Adenauer in 1956 thought the loveliest thing he had ever seen.

The house itself is in use as a very desirable lunch venue, where the clink of glasses and hum of convivial conversation drift down over the heads of the plant hunters and the holidaymakers on the walks below. This is a pleasant little island world, a short escape from the mundane, to which every garden-lover should one day pay a visit. And however dodgy her story, the visitor would probably never have come here at all but for the enterprising spirit of Antoinette Bayer, who imagined herself Baroness St Leger in her own little dream world on a sunny island in a lake.

funds to run a first-class show. This is a model of how it can be done.

The garden seen today is quite clearly the descendant of the St Leger garden, complete with its Emden improvements. It is greatly to the credit of the present management that it still has the character of a private garden – something very difficult to achieve under a collective form of ownership. There is a winding circuit walk round the shore of the whole rather elongated island of Isola Grande during which there are sufficient corners of rocky solitude for the visitor to have those little Robinson Crusoe moments that must have been precious to the owners of the past.

But this suggestion of the simple life soon gives way to something more sumptuous. The old lawns with their

ABOVE *Lapageria rosea*, a lovely climber and the national flower of Chile, seldom shows its dusky pink flowers outdoors in Europe. On the pergola here, however, it looks perfectly at home.

ABOVE Any botanic garden would be proud of this display of southern-hemisphere shrubs. In the foreground is *Protea grandiceps* from South Africa, among specimens of its near and far relations.

LAKE COMO

PART TWO

LAKE COMO

Lying only a short distance north of the great city of Milan, the business capital of Italy, Lake Como should have been overrun by inappropriate development and tourist tat many years ago, but it is not so. The reason for this is its dramatic geography: its mountainous flanks rise steeply from its shores to form a sort of inland fjord emerging from the wall of the Alps. Green forests of sweet chestnut (*Castanea sativa*) hang from its slopes, and the great crags rise above them, snow-capped in winter and fringed with uncertain clouds throughout the year. The nature of the gorge makes the climate changeable, with the weather shifting unpredictably, so that yachts are seldom to be seen on Lake Como. The shores are steep and rocky, providing few sites for settlement, and progress along the perimeter roads is slow. All this has meant that the lake has remained a place for the romantic pilgrim rather than the casual pleasure-seeker.

The earliest recorded visitor to describe his experience here was Pliny the Younger in the first century CE. Like his uncle, Pliny the Elder, he came from the Roman city of Como, at the south-western tip of the lake. Here, the first Roman emperor, Augustus, maintained a fleet of six galleys ready to repel incursions from the tribes to the north. Pliny the Younger, the very man who in his youth described the eruption of Vesuvius which destroyed Pompeii, became a considerable grandee in later life. He had a string of luxurious residences across Italy and modern Turkey, where he was a governor. He was vitally interested in gardens, and two of his surviving letters give us our best descriptions of patrician Roman villa gardens.

Pliny the Younger always remained attached to the scenery of his birthplace, and maintained at least two villas on the shores of Lake Como. One of these, called Tragœdia after the raised shoes worn by Roman tragic actors, was sited high up, to command a view of the lake; very likely, it was on the peninsula at Bellagio – the scenic focal point of the lake. Pliny the Younger described how the villa overlooked the lake and the fishermen below, just in the way that the windows of Bellagio's belle-époque hotels now look out on fishing boats winding in the silver *lavarello* or, with big reels mounted on the stern, the delicious char (*salmerino*) from far below in a lake which is one of the deepest in Europe.

OPPOSITE The contrast between brilliant floral terraces in the foreground and the brooding mystery of the lake beyond is very characteristic of Lake Como, where the constantly changing weather conditions are an endless source of fascination.

Pliny the Younger's other villa, Comœdia, occupied the site of the later Villa Pliniana in an isolated cove near Torno. The present villa, built in the 1570s, matches Pliny's assertion that 'you can fish from it yourself, casting your line from your bedroom window and practically from your bed as if you were in a boat'. This site has always been associated with the ebbing and flowing spring investigated by many visitors, including Leonardo da Vinci in 1498.

The golden age of Lake Como's European fame came in the Romantic era at the end of the eighteenth century. In 1793, the young William Wordsworth was here, fresh from his mixed experiences during the revolution in France. His response to Lake Como was a long poem with the typically uninformative title *Descriptive Sketches*, nowadays relegated to the introductory juvenilia of his collected works but bearing the unmistakable mark of genius. In his wake, seeking the elemental power of nature, came a stream of writers, composers and grandees, building their elegant villas on the lake shore. Lord Byron and Percy Bysshe Shelley were here, and the hero of Stendhal's novel *The Charterhouse of Parma* set out on his adventures from his home on Lake Como.

Stendhal summed up the romantic mood in his journal entry for 18 July 1817:

This morning at five o'clock we left Como in a boat covered with a beautiful blue and white canopy. We visited the villa of the Princess of Wales and the Pliniana with its intermittent fountain; Pliny's letter is engraved in the marble. At this point the lake becomes wild and sombre: the mountains drop down almost sheer into the water. We rounded the point of Balbianello, not without difficulty, and the ladies were afraid: it was as rugged a sight as that of the Scottish lakes. At last we caught sight of the Tremezzina shore and of those charming little valleys which, protected to the north by a high mountain, enjoy a climate like that at Rome. Those Milanese who suffer from the cold come to spend the winter here. The palaces become numerous along the green slopes and are reflected in the water . . . they are built in an elegant, picturesque, voluptuous style . . .

the sound of bells, mellowed by the distance and
the wavelets of the lake, find an echo in suffering
souls. How can I describe this emotion? One must
love the arts: one must love and be unhappy.

As Stendhal struggled with his feelings and pressed on to
find his spirits revived by visiting gardens, others around
him were equally stimulated. Gioachino Rossini composed
Tancredi here in 1813, and Vincenzo Bellini wrote *La
Sonnambula* and *Norma*, two of the enduring bel-canto
operas, at the Villa Passalacqua in Moltrasio. For *Norma*,
Bellini had the great soprano of the day, Giuditta Pasta
(imagine an Italian soprano called Madame Pasta!), installed
in a villa in Como so as to be on call as the great work
unfolded. We can imagine the day when the first sound
of Bellini and Pasta tentatively practising 'Casta Diva'
drifted out of an open window and down to the lake. Later,
Giuseppe Verdi wrote part of *La Traviata* nearby in 1853, and
Franz Liszt carried on an enthusiastic affair at Bellagio, one
result of which was the birth of his daughter Cosima, famous
now as the wife of Richard Wagner.

Alongside these noble outpourings, great events were stirring
on the shores of Lake Como. During the nineteenth century,
the decisive struggle which changed Italy from a jigsaw
puzzle of miniature principalities and de-facto colonies into
the modern nation state took place, and this was the front
line. Two of Napoleon Bonaparte's right-hand men in his
political manipulation of Italy – Francesco Melzi d'Eril and
Gian Battista Sommariva – established themselves in lakeside
villas with important gardens on opposite sides of the lake,
at Bellagio and Tremezzo respectively. Each was engaged in
a silent status contest with his rival. After Bonaparte's fall
in 1815, Lake Como, being part of Lombardy, came under
Austrian rule.

The definitive novel of the Risorgimento, Alessandro
Manzoni's *I Promessi Sposi* [The Betrothed], published in
1827, opens on the Lecco branch of the lake: the book was

ABOVE The shore of Lake Como rises steeply from the surface, providing
few opportunities for extensive building plots. Villa gardens are laid out
on terraces, providing romantic scenery for travellers on the lake. In the
background, the slopes are typically forested.

intended as a call to national awakening, and was written
in a carefully constructed form of Italian intended to serve
as the standard language when the great day dawned. Silvio
Pellico, one of the early heroes of the unification movement,
was dramatically arrested by the Austrian authorities at the
Villa del Balbianello, famous then and now for its sensational
garden setting on the lake. Patrician supporters of the
movement, forbidden to display symbols of their nationalist
views, took to planting strawberry trees (*Arbutus unedo*) at
their gates. The tree is evergreen, and bears its white flowers
and red fruits at the same time, thus combining the three
colours of the revolutionary flag. When Giuseppe Garibaldi's
redshirt volunteers finally took Como in 1859, the great
man commandeered a pleasure steamer and sailed up and
down the lake flying that flag and firing guns to launch the
general insurrection.

After Italian unification in 1861, life began to settle down.
The numbers of seasonal visitors on the lake rose steadily,
and Bellagio and Cadenabbia were soon adorned by hotels
catering for an expensive clientele. They often arrived in
spring, a particularly lovely time on the lake, as a sort of
finale to a winter spent on the French Riviera.

A splendid villa built in 1854 on the prime plot of land on the

tip of the promontory at Bellagio was extended into a hotel
after a generation, and continues its glittering reputation as
the Grand Hotel Villa Serbelloni. Further south is the Villa
D'Este at Cernobbio, the former residence of George IV's
estranged wife, and it is now also a splendidly old-school
hotel which retains its very interesting historic garden. By
the time the enjoyably cynical Richard Bagot's standard
book *The Italian Lakes* was published in 1905, he was able to
complain that: 'unluckily Cadenabbia may be said to have
been annexed by the English and Americans . . . in the spring
and autumn seasons. Tea-parties and gossip, and an intensely
British atmosphere of the type savouring of evensong
and the parish magazine reign supreme in Cadenabbia at
these times.'

He recommended the fastidious visitor to arrive, like himself,
by carriage rather than train, in order to avoid 'the guttural

ABOVE The little town of Bellagio, remote on its long peninsula between
the two branches of the lake, lies at the foot of the wooded hill which
forms the park of the Villa Serbelloni. The mountain shore of the Lecco
branch looms behind.

OPPOSITE Where space can be found, as here at the Villa del Balbianello, all
that is needed is a skilful and knowing hand to form garden foregrounds
of simple beauty. The climate will do the rest.

and nasal exclamations of admiration from Germans and
Americans, or vapid expressions of enthusiasm from British
fellow-travellers'. The fact was that Bagot was deeply
attached to Lake Como, which he knew intimately, and his
apparent resentment of superficial visitors was assuaged
by the comfortable income he deservedly earned from the
several editions of his travelogue over the next twenty years.
The world of Bagot's pre-war bourgeoisie, stepping off
landing stages on slow boats to lakeside garden picnics, is
cleverly evoked by Gladys Huntington's remarkable novel
Madame Solario, published anonymously in 1956 but set
convincingly in a Cadenabbia grand hotel fifty years earlier.
After Italy's appalling experience in the First World War,
tenderly evoked by memorials such as the bronze Alpino
in the square at Lenno, the old order was no more.
Several significant properties were bought by wealthy and
enterprising Americans. These included the Villa Serbelloni,
occupying most of the wooded promontory at Bellagio,
acquired in 1928 by the whisky heiress Ella Walker, and the
equally famous Villa del Balbianello, projecting into the

lake near Lenno, whose purchase by Butler Ames is a story
in itself. Both these acquisitions were staging posts on the
route to eventual public access to the respective gardens in
modern times.

The garden visitor to Lake Como today finds the scenery
surprisingly similar to that depicted and venerated by past
admirers. The great lake, made to seem narrow by the
towering mountains rising on all sides, flows south from the
Valtellina and divides in two at the Punta Spartivento [point
at which the wind divides] at Bellagio. The western branch,
its banks sprinkled with villas and dotted with villages,
proceeds south past the wooded promontory of Balbianello
and the solitary island of Isola Comacina, towards the city
of Como, whence the seaplane club sends out its craft,
distinctively droning over the lake on sunny afternoons. The
eastern branch flows down the relatively silent and lonely

ABOVE Part of the pleasure of the visitor experience at the Villa Sommi
Picenardi is the unexpected mingling of intimacy with grandeur. Here, a
glimpse through a planted arch reveals the terraced garden beyond.

gorge towards Lecco, with a railway line along the shore connecting the industrial city of Lecco with the Moto Guzzi motorcycle factory and museum at Mandello del Lario and the pretty lakeside village of Varenna, a favourable base for garden visiting.

Always remember that the weather is fickle around Lake Como, so that a strong wind pushing south from the Alps can be suddenly succeeded by a memorable flat calm. The level of the lake varies dramatically from year to year and from season to season. The many contrary winds characteristic of the lake are typically shown, complete with names, on local maps.

The microclimate allows a wide range of garden vegetation to be grown here, but the overall pattern is noticeably harsher than on Lake Maggiore. The soil is typically alkaline,

derived from the limestone geology so spectacularly displayed along the Tremezzina shore, but some major gardens have overlaid this with imported acid soil in a successful attempt to cultivate the woodland garden flora of the *Rhododendron* and *Camellia*.

In the centre of the lake around Bellagio there is plenty of charming lodging available, and in neighbouring Menaggio and Cadenabbia. The public service boats keep up a regular and frequent service to and from the landing stages. Each is a pleasant walk from a garden destination, though really you should arrive by boat at the steps of the Villa del Balbianello. In the towns and villages themselves, there is sufficient variety of tourist fare and local tradition to satisfy both the casual visitor and the cultural connoisseur, who should of course eat the fish or risotto of the day and wash it down with the hearty wines of the Valtellina. However, the real, enduring pleasure of Lake Como comes from simply gazing out from the innumerable vantage points at the sublime spectacle of the gleaming lake in its many moods, and letting the eye run up to the often snow-capped peaks, edged and rimmed with tufts of cloud, in this very special place.

BELOW Though the *Lariana*, shown on page 9, is long gone, her sister craft the *Milano* still plies the lake. Here, she approaches the Dosso di Lavedo near Lenno. The highest peak of the central mountains, Monte San Primo, can be seen, dusted with snow.

VILLA MELZI

Most of the elegant villa gardens along the shore of Lake Como can only be viewed tantalisingly from a passing boat as they cannot be visited by the paying public. The Villa Melzi is a spectacular exception to this, its gates standing open at all reasonable hours for a modest fee. The easy walk from the centre of Bellagio along the Lungolago adds to the feeling of a civilized arrangement. The house was built, and its grounds laid out, around 1810 for Francesco Melzi d'Eril, whose life and achievements exemplify the principles and ultimate fate of the Enlightenment in Italy. Melzi came from a patrician Milanese background. His life's work was spent in politics, trying to achieve a new settlement of liberal, constitutional government against a backdrop of fragmentation and absolutism. This new dawn of a society organized along rational lines, with the decrees of despots tempered by a progressive outlook and gentlemanly discussion, was swept aside in the wake of the French Revolution, but Melzi managed to ride out the storm, retire with his dignity reasonably intact and live out the quiet life of the elder statesman in this magnificent setting.

When Bonaparte's army swept across the Alps and conquered Lombardy in 1796, he established a short-lived statelet in northern Italy called the Cisalpine Republic. Melzi, seen as a safe pair of hands, was given high office in this outfit. Later, when the conquest of the peninsula was complete, the Republic of Italy was created. Melzi was appointed vice-president, with only the great man above

him. His moment had finally arrived, his victory sweetened by the fact that the defeated rival candidate was Gian Battista Sommariva, whose luxury residence, now the Villa Carlotta, was straight across the lake from Melzi's property. Soon, however, Bonaparte's republican ideals were jettisoned in that famous moment when he crowned himself emperor in Paris and assumed also the subsidiary title of king of Italy. With the new regime of robes and thrones, Melzi found his services no longer required. He was given the splendid but pointless title of duke of Lodi and went back to his Lombard roots. He remained proud, however, of his brief period of brilliance, and there is a real sense of Napoleonic consequence on show at the Villa Melzi.

Melzi made an unconventional choice as his architect, the Milanese *stuccatore* Giocondo Albertolli. Albertolli put up a neat white block as the centrepiece of the layout, a cool piece of neoclassicism relying on proportion and clean lines rather than exterior show, as it were to announce to the world that this is the home of a man of refinement and seemly restraint. A columned portico was debated, but eventually rejected. Albertolli also designed the Melzi chapel at the San Giovanni end of the garden.

Around these structures, a garden in the English landscape style was formed, smoothly trowelled over the ancient terraces, with a calm network of gently swirling gravel walks leading the visitor through the landform of rounded greenery. Groves of trees were placed at elegant intervals, and garden pavilions in an eclectic range of styles punctuated the route at strategic points like scenes from the unfolding plot of a minor opera.

It is something of a curiosity that Melzi should have chosen the English style of garden design for his lasting contribution

OPPOSITE A putto gives a dolphin a hard time in the little formal garden in front of the house. Beyond, the shadowy form of the Dosso di Lavedo, the wooded grounds of the Villa del Balbianello, can be made out.

to cultural history when he was a leading figure in a
government at war with Britain for so many years. There are
two reasonable explanations. Firstly, the landscape style, with
its polite emulation of natural forms, represented a liberal
outlook, in contrast to the bold geometry of the baroque
style, which reached its flood tide at the Versailles of Louis
XIV and can thus be seen as the emblem of absolutism.
To this political undercurrent we can add the second
explanation – the powerful attraction of fashion. Napoleon's
own brother, Louis, installed as king of Holland, converted
the controlling baroque grid of the garden at his hunting
palace of Het Loo, near Apeldoorn, to the open lawns and

ABOBVE The form of the Villa Melzi's garden is best seen from a boat on
the lake. The rounded lawns, artfully scattered with trees and shrubs,
announce the estate of an enlightened gentleman.

RIGHT The lake façade of the Villa Melzi looks straight across the water
towards the historically rival establishment, the Villa Carlotta, at the foot
of the mighty Monte di Tremezzo.

OPPOSITE ABOVE The Villa Melzi commands magnificent views. Here,
looking southward along the Como branch of the lake, a pair of columns
frames the view of Balbianello.

OPPOSITE BELOW There is plenty of variety to be seen in the grounds. Here,
a *Rhododendron* grows freely alongside trimmed blobs of related species,
novelty topiary in a land much addicted to such things

serpentine lines of the English style. (It was returned to its golden-age glitter only in the 1980s.) Melzi's new layout could thus be presented as being in the van of elegant fashion rather than a waspish political statement. Nonetheless, the landscape style was ideally suited to an Enlightenment outlook, suggesting a gentleman at ease with the world, strolling in his elegant grounds, in tune with a range of sophisticated and progressive ideas, rejecting the twin threats of despotism and ignorance as rather beneath his notice. The garden was designed, or at least its plan drawn, by Luigi Canonica and Luigi Villoresi at the same time as the house. The English landscape garden had made a late arrival in Italy, though once it got there it became very popular.

It is likely that the Villa Melzi garden was an early trendsetter. The first Italian book on the subject, Ercole Silva's *Dell'Arte dei Giardini Inglesi* [The Art of English Gardens], was published only in 1801, with an amplified second edition in 1813. Silva (whose name translates pleasantly as Hercules Wood, like a gardener from a novel) came from Lombardy and made his own garden in the new style there, so it is likely

Melzi was familiar with his work both in print and on the ground. Given the assured style of everything seen at the Villa Melzi, this was a very promising beginning.

The walk through the grounds begins at its quietly placed gates on the lake shore. One of the gate piers announces the various titles of Francesco Melzi d'Eril, and leaves the visitor to wonder whether it is just a coincidence that Leonardo da Vinci's chief assistant, to whom he left all his property and effects at his death, bore the same name. The walk progresses calmly along the shore, under big shady groves of ornamental

ABOVE From the upper parts of the grounds, the simple white form of the villa, decorated with its entertaining selection of chimney stacks, begins to form a foreground to the noble scenery of the lake.

OPPOSITE ABOVE The line of pollarded planes (*Platanus*) along the shoreline walk reminds the visitor of Franz Liszt's extended stay in Bellagio. He composed under these trees between assignations with Madame d'Agoult.

OPPOSITE BELOW The Moorish kiosk is the first of the garden buildings encountered by the visitor entering the grounds from Bellagio. Its design reflects the Moorish taste fashionable in the early nineteenth century.

trees dating from the second half of the nineteenth century. Gradually the visitor becomes aware of the swelling lawns rising on the left, crowned with groups of pink azaleas (*Rhododendron*). These lawns are studded with primroses in spring. I pointed them out with a smile one day to a gardener busily engaged nearby. He glanced at them, shrugged and apologized: 'We just have not got the staff.' My wild flowers were his weeds. Lady Fortescue had a similar conversation with her native gardener in *Perfume from Provence*.

LEFT There are plenty of quiet spots for the reveries of the solitary walker at the Villa Melzi. In spring, paths with a surface like a Roman road invite the visitor to stroll among the flowering *Rhododendron* and the groves of evergreen trees.

BELOW The cleverly handled landform offers alternative routes for repeat visitors, each skilfully engineered to suggest spontaneity while providing easy walking, and all offering a variety of views.

Soon the visitor reaches the first of the ornamental buildings – a Moorish kiosk perched right on the edge of the lake, with a little balcony-for-two suspended over the water. This is a style that was very popular in the early nineteenth century, reflecting the international vogue typified by Washington Irving's romantically vague *Tales of the Alhambra* of 1832. From within the kiosk, three framed views of the lake shore are seen, in just the style prescribed in the Picturesque fashion of the day: one straight across to the mountain above Tremezzo; another south to the silhouetted hump of Balbianello; and a third along to the shoreline to Bellagio, with the Alps towering behind.

Looking back into the garden, another literary icon is outlined by the doorway. It is a double statue of Beatrice leading Dante out of purgatory to paradise. When Franz Liszt came to Bellagio in 1837, he conducted an enthusiastic affair with Madame d'Agoult, resulting in the birth of their daughter Cosima, later to become famous in musical circles for rather different reasons. Liszt's swirling emotions were given some relief by sitting in the shade of the plane (*Platanus*) tree walk at the Villa Melzi, where he composed his sonata *Après une Lecture de Dante*.

The walk then continues to the garden in front of the house – the only geometric part of the ornamental layout. The steps to the house are flanked by a wonderful piece of classical simplicity: two long shallow swags of ivy (*Hedera*), perfectly placed on sloping lawns. Melzi is here linking himself with Virgil, who described in the *Georgics* how Roman farmers trained vines in swags between evenly spaced elm (*Ulmus*) trees; the ornamental effect was used and described by Pliny the Younger, when he trained ivy between plane trees in his garden.

A simple level rectangle pushes out into a semicircular terrace commanding a view of the lake, from Lenno along the length of the famous Tremezzina shore, lined with villas in various styles and colours. Behind are the overwhelming mountains with their tilted geology and thinly scattered shepherds' huts. It is impossible to ignore the blinding

ABOVE RIGHT The statue group of Dante and Beatrice attracted Mark Twain's attention on his visit. This wood engraving in his *Innocents Abroad* of 1869 shows how little has changed since his time.

RIGHT A little more enclosed nowadays, perhaps, but Dante's imaginary girlfriend continues to show the way forward today. The statue group, commemorating Liszt's visits here, stands by the Moorish kiosk.

white square of Sommariva's rival establishment at the Villa Carlotta loudly announcing itself across the water. The status contest between the two establishments is unmistakable. On the shoreline below the terrace is an ingenious effect. Artificial stalactites are placed along the rocky 'beach', generating a picturesque effect. No doubt, they are intended to prevent pleasure-seekers drawing up their boats for a spontaneous look in.

Having walked past the house, the visitor soon comes to an open lawn framed by handsome trees and shrubs. On the left is a giant metal basket surrounding a flower bed superbly modelled into the turf, very much in the manner of Humphry Repton's work in England in the early nineteenth century. The gentle rise and fall of this lawn, so carefully artless, is a masterpiece in itself.

The next objective is the chapel. This offers some relief from the inevitable disappointment of not being permitted to view the interior of the house, as the architect is the same, and there is fine work within. The little white building on a Greek cross plan, placed at the Loppia entrance to the garden, is adorned inside with a wonderful combination of stuccowork

and grisaille painting, so good in each instance that the eye has some difficulty telling which is which. There are three good monuments, one of which shows Francesco Melzi d'Eril in medallion profile, mourned by a despondent young woman and an equally miserable lion, his body language clearly modelled on a favourite dog. Below, the relief face of a sarcophagus shows, either side of various disconsolate characters of all ranks and ages, two personifications of Fame blowing their respective trumpets. In a very different style, the nearby memorial to the moustachioed Duke

BELOW There are magnificent views north along the lake from the garden. Here, the picturesque townscape of Bellagio leads the eye on to the great peaks at the northern end of Lake Como, their tops crowned with snow in spring.

OPPOSITE ABOVE Quiet walks along solitary winding paths are a pensive pleasure at the Villa Melzi. The curious stiffness of the trimmed evergreen blobs is relieved here and there by the occasional free-growing specimen, such as this *Mahonia*.

OPPOSITE BELOW The great white orangery near the house, now used as an exhibition space, is set among giant *Jubaea* palms from Chile, lending an exotic air to the view across the lake and its framing mountains.

Lodovico of 1886 features a full-length effigy of him framed in a magnificent representation of heavy folds of curtain fabric, complete with convincing tassels, in gleaming black marble. The more you look, the better it is.

The walk now leads, via a magnificent screen of bamboo underplanted with *Aspidistra*, along a raised terrace behind the house to the big white orangery. Its vegetable contents are long gone, but it is easy to imagine them being wheeled out after the frosts to form a forest of shining green standards along the terrace. The orangery is now filled with an interesting display centred around Francesco Melzi d'Eril's brief period of Napoleonic glory, including a photograph of his rather collectable letterhead as vice-president of the Italian Republic. The letter itself, addressed to Napoleon, begins with the memorable phrase '*Citoyen Président . . .*' Next to it is a drawing of a proposed medallion bearing the twin heads, in receding profile, of Napoleon and Melzi.

If time permits, it is worth taking a short excursion up the hill to see the range of nineteenth-century, curvilinear glasshouses in the former kitchen garden. These are an impressive survival, and though some have been reglazed they form a fine group, probably of the 1840s, designed on the principles of iron and glass technology developed in Britain by J.C. Loudon. Here the buildings step handsomely

ABOVE The stiffly recumbent classical lions keep guard at the entrance to the villa, adorned by the great swags of ivy (*Hedera*). The shady walk of planes (*Platanus*) leads the eye back to the Bellagio gate.

OPPOSITE ABOVE From the garden, a detailed panorama opens up a little further south along the lake shore, focused on the elegant Palladian-revival Villa Trivulzio next door, cleverly placed for maximum effect.

OPPOSITE BELOW Light and shade effects are subtle in the garden in spring. In the foreground, mixed azaleas (*Rhododendron*) break into flower, while their heavyweight counterparts begin to catch up beyond. Big trees define the character at every season.

down a south-facing slope on a series of terraces. The glasshouses are still used for their original purpose.

From the orangery the visitor returns gradually to the Bellagio entrance, passing under wonderful groups of super-tall tulip (*Liriodendron tulipifera*) and maidenhair (*Ginkgo biloba*) trees before descending to the Japanese garden laid out in the 1950s. Here delicate maples (*Acer*), *Hosta* and little bridges frame shapely pools, just before the visitor walks out through the chunky grotto, a place for shade on hot days. On top of the grotto, an artifically ruined Gothick gateway can be seen. This gave access to the park above the garden. The park is not open to the public, but can be viewed to advantage from a passing boat on the lake, from which the position of the house and garden, slung elegantly in the saddle between the Bellagio promontory and the mountains to the south, is best appreciated.

LEFT Those in search of horticultural detail will find it in the relatively modern Japanese-themed garden near the entrance. The multicoloured crowns of mixed Japanese maples (*Acer*) lean over a curvaceous pool with big groups of *Hosta* along its banks.

ABOVE The elegant little bridge in the Japanese garden has lovely groups of royal fern (*Osmunda regalis*) at either end, revelling in the cool shady conditions. It needs its feet in the water, as here.

VILLA CARLOTTA

The Villa Carlotta and its long flanking garden terraces create a striking impression on the approach by boat across Lake Como. Three paintings in the house make it clear that the visitor is expected to arrive this way, rather than by the narrow and awkward lakeside road. Although the site has undergone a series of changes of ownership and garden style over three centuries, it has taken all this in its stride and retained its status as the great destination on the lake.

The villa was built at the end of the seventeenth century for the Clerici family, who had risen from rural origins here to rich and powerful silk merchants. By the time the house was commissioned, they were established as politicians, aristocrats and power brokers in Milan, where their town house – the Palazzo Clerici – was acquired from a branch of the ubiquitously influential Visconti dynasty. The choice of site for the villa on Lake Como seems to have been motivated by ancestral family landholdings on the lake shore. Marchese Giorgio II Clerici's country estate was complete in its initial form by 1695. The garden is first mentioned in 1699, when the French influence emanating from the Versailles of Louis XIV radiated across Europe.

The site, as so often on Lake Como, is awkward, because the land rises steeply from the shore. The initial view of the house from the forecourt is liable to generate a crick in the neck as it towers precipitously above the eyeline. It has always

been so. The designer of a baroque house and garden would naturally prefer a long axial approach – the longer the better – but this is impossible here, so height has been wielded instead to deliver the initial shock to the visitor's composure. Meanwhile, the garden extends along apparently endless terraces to either side of the house. The baroque gardener wishes to subjugate nature, but that could never be achieved here, where the terraces, and especially the house, act instead as a platform to admire the epic scenery. No visitor to the interior of the house should miss the early decorative painted timberwork on the ceilings of several of the rooms, simply covered over during later remodellings and rediscovered in recent years. All this early work, overlaid but not destroyed by later developments, continues to define the character of the estate.

The Clerici continued their rise up the social scale during the eighteenth century, and reached the height of their glory during the life of Marchese Anton Giorgio Clerici (1715–68), general of artillery and ambassador for the Holy Roman Emperor and knight of the Golden Fleece. He commissioned Giambattista Tiepolo's sensational ceiling fresco in the Milan town house, and spent lavishly on his lakeside retreat. Marcantonio Dal Re's engravings of 1743 show a fountain at the lake entrance, with twirly box (*Buxus*) parterres laid out on either side of the house. Visitors climbing the great staircase towards the house were liable to be showered from above and below with jets of water without warning. The contrast between the giant elongated steps of the terracing and the heroic mountain scenery rising behind them serves to a modern eye only to emphasize the effort of human achievement dwarfed by the nobility of creation.

OPPOSITE The visitor's first view of the house is this startling image from the little parterre within the gate. The house rises cliff-like dead ahead, with everything leading the eye to the centre of the building.

Magnificent personalities are often impossible to follow, and
within a generation the Clerici had left the villa. In 1801,
Anton Giorgio's only daughter, Claudia Biglia Clerici, herself
childless, sold the property to Gian Battista Sommariva.
Sommariva was a new kind of large-scale actor on the
European stage, one of the ruthless self-made men who
had made the most of the Napoleonic reorganization
following his startling conquests. Unlike his rival, the
patrician Francesco Melzi d'Eril across the lake at Villa Melzi,
Sommariva began as a barber's apprentice in Milan and rose
to establish himself as Bonaparte's key man of affairs in
northern Italy. His bust in the entrance hall shows him in the
full glory of the *arriviste*: a larger-than-life, white marble bust
with luxuriant curly hair and a Roman toga. His very name,
Sommariva, suggests his recent appearance on the scene.
He gazes out challengingly at the Villa Melzi, glinting far
below on the opposite shore, where the visitor can imagine

OPPOSITE ABOVE The improbable image of a palm tree rising above *Rhododendron* set against an Alpine lake and forest scenery is all part of the fun at the Villa Carlotta.

OPPOSITE BELOW Jean Joseph-Xavier Bidauld's 1819 view of the then Villa Sommariva from the lake shows the garden terraces extending evenly to either side of the house.

ABOVE New blooms spread across the domes and crowns of *Rhododendron* on the undulating lawns of the Villa Carlotta. Across the lake, the historical rival establishment of the Villa Melzi twinkles on the shore.

the owner cringing at the unexpected consequences of the new order.

Sommariva gave his new trophy house a makeover to bring it into line with the neoclassical taste of the early nineteenth century. The form of the house was left substantially intact, but given a greater central emphasis on the lake front by the addition of balconies to address the famous view. The most surprising change, however, is the prominent clock face sticking up like a topknot, surely confirmation to Melzi that the new man was not quite the thing.

Yet it would be wrong to write off Sommariva as a mere poseur: he was a key patron of the great sculptors of the day,

RIGHT Under a pergola, in the shade of the big trees, comfortable benches await the itinerant view-taker. In these gardens, there must always be a happy balance between seeking out the prize specimen and taking time to consider the wider setting.

BELOW In the reverse view, the rococo box (*Buxus*) scrolls delicately frame the central pond. The letter C for Carlotta is repeated in the lovely ironwork of the gates, framing the view east across the lake.

ABOVE The troublesome little fountain putto teases a jet of water out
of the dolphin's mouth in front of the dramatic series of staircases and
balconies on the approach.

Antonio Canova and Bertel Thorwaldsen. Among the many choice Napoleonic items on display in the house is the frieze depicting the entry of Alexander the Great into Babylon. This had been ordered by Napoleon for the Panthéon in Paris, but never reached its destination when the great man was overthrown, and poor Thorwaldsen was left with it filling his studio. Sommariva, who stood by Bonaparte at the fall, bought the frieze, had himself (full length, in a toga) added to the end of the frieze, and the whole thing installed in the entrance hall of the villa, where it remains. He also

ABOVE There is no end of visual entertainment on the level terrace north of the house. Here, an annual planting of mature cacti in every shape and form is convincingly worked in among the weathered stones of a naturalistic rock garden.

RIGHT The otherworldly form of *Dasylirion* reaches out above a charmingly naturalized group of the terrestrial orchid *Bletilla*.

added the domed family chapel and mausoleum by the lake shore, next to the modern visitor entrance. This chapel remains in the family ownership.

Sommariva seems to have left the framework of the terraced gardens essentially intact, but an early nineteenth-century engraving based on a drawing by his daughter-in-law Emilia Seillère Sommariva shows a romantic park in the English style rising behind the house. While this may be something of an elaboration of what was actually achieved, there was once a Temple of Friendship as the focal point of this backdrop of walks and groves above the formal garden. The Sommariva family's fortunes also waned, and the estate was bought, in 1843, by Princess Marianne of the Netherlands, the wife of Prince Albrecht of Prussia. In 1847,

LEFT *Aurinia saxatilis* and a lilac *Phlox* spread and hang over the carefully placed strata of the rock garden.

BELOW The planting on the rock garden is an unexpected mixture of the perennial with the annual. Pansies (*Viola*), double daisies (*Bellis*) and orange wallflowers (*Erysimum*) vie for attention in a sort of floral landslide.

OVERLEAF The sublime and the ridiculous are readily found side by side on the main terrace. The startling melange of blinding colours on the rock garden, piled on afresh each year, is a foreground to the *Wisteria* which has climbed right up a pine tree.

she gave it to her daughter, Charlotte, on the occasion of her marriage to Georg, heir to the dukedom of Saxe-Meiningen. Charlotte's name was readily Italianized to Carlotta – hence the present name of the villa. The gilded letter C, with its hovering coronet, on the gates at the forecourt entrance, recalls Charlotte rather than the ancestral Clerici as is often assumed. Charlotte herself was a granddaughter of the famous beauty Queen Luise of Prussia, and thus related to her namesake, Queen Charlotte, wife of George III of England. The marriage was a love match, but short-lived: Charlotte died in childbirth in 1855, at the age of twenty-three. Georg's two subsequent marriages did not match the promise of the first. He consoled himself by becoming a considerable patron of the arts, notably of the music of Johannes Brahms.

The Saxe-Meiningen era brought a change of style which continues to define the garden of the Villa Carlotta. The present forecourt, with its distinctive fountain in the centre of a little box (*Buxus*) parterre, was retained as it had been during the Sommariva years. From an early stage, however, the long terraces were richly replanted in the newly fashionable English style of the woodland garden. While the level walks made for easy promenading, the slopes rising above them were transformed into undulating lawns studded with ornamental trees and shrubs. In mid-spring, the visitor now sees sheets of brilliant azaleas (*Rhododendron*) everywhere, with pines, *Magnolia* and planes (*Platanus*) towering over them. The sight of the azaleas is a surprise, though visible from afar: the geology of Lake Como is limestone, but the topsoil is acid, brought in great quantities

BELOW LEFT On the winding upper walks, the rich variety of *Rhododendron* foliage forms a foreground to their flowers framed among the trees.
BELOW RIGHT The stream flows down the valley of tree ferns (*Dicksonia*), providing a refreshing contrast to some of the floral excitement. The tree ferns themselves are planted out here each spring in their big pots.
OPPOSITE The taste of the nineteenth-century garden maker required variety in all things: plant shape, leaf colour, landform, light and shade. The search for richness and contrast is well exemplified in this garden.

from elsewhere to furnish the necessary growing medium. Such mind-blowing extravagance is quite normal in these subalpine gardens, as it is on the similarly stony slopes of the Riviera.

Duke Georg's long life came conveniently to an end at the outbreak of the First World War, in 1914. The following year, Italy entered the war and found itself allied against Germany, so the Villa Carlotta was now the property of an enemy alien. The villa was not in fact confiscated but placed under temporary management, but the family were never likely to return in the changed circumstances after the war. In 1922, the estate was to be sold at auction, but local enthusiasts intervened and held it until 1927, when the present owners – a charitable trust – took charge.

When looking down today from the central balcony, the little parterre can be seen, set in a giant grove of *Camellia*, no doubt once freely billowing but now clipped as a sort of monster hedge. The *Camellia* are studded with pink and white in early spring. In the early warmth of mid-spring, the rising terraces reveal a succession of trickling grottoes,

LEFT Sometimes nature has its own ideas, with magnificent results. The dragon-like trunk of a mighty *Wisteria* has hauled itself up a big pine tree, presenting an extraordinary spectacle against the pretty backdrop of spring-flowering shrubs.

ABOVE Cool serpentine walks, lined with mondo grass (*Ophiopogon japonicus*), work their way through the shady *Rhododendron* groves in many parts of the garden.

curtains of *Rosa banksiae* 'Lutea' – its blooms impossibly plump, soft and fragrant in the spring air – and superlative bedding on the top level. There, brilliant colour-graded planting in beds is enhanced by regularly spaced, terracotta pots, with invitingly elegant, dark green timber benches between. Any suggestion of municipal tedium is immediately dispelled by the sheer quality of the work, which is fresh and pretty in spring and handsomely blowsy in autumn. Along

OPPOSITE ABOVE A surprising sight from the upper floor of the house is this neat little scrollwork parterre of box (*Buxus*), placed at a steep gradient to face the viewer. It stands directly above a little grotto.
OPPOSITE BELOW The view from the terraces at the Villa Carlotta is squarely across the lake at the former rival establishment of the Villa Melzi at Bellagio. The stiffness of the past is now replaced by mutual admiration.
ABOVE The upper balconies of the house give a precipitous view of the garden entrance below. The parterre now seems tiny, walled in by clipped monster hedges of *Camellia* and cherry laurel (*Prunus laurocerasus*).

one terrace, a pergola of oranges and lemons (*Citrus* × *limon*) shades the walk. Of course, you cannot grow lemons out of doors in the Alps, so these are cunningly glazed in for the winter. It is a pleasant deception.

The long terraces lead away on either side from the back of the house. Heading north, the visitor is constantly offered a choice between easy promenading on the broad gravel walk and the diverting alternatives: up into the valley of ferns, where, each spring, tree ferns (*Dicksonia*) are planted into a cool shady ravine watered by a cascading stream; down into the maze of narrow walks, lined by azaleas (*Rhododendron*) rising above the eyeline, towards the shore and the range of former glasshouses, now serving as a secluded café; or the visitor could go on along the main walk, soon to be confronted by a rock garden planted in the most startling mixture of seasonal colours. A great *Wisteria* climbs to the top of a pine on a sloping lawn, and nearby great specimens of *Magnolia grandiflora* – a favourite tree of northern Italian

gardens – are handsomely dotted about. This is just the sort of planting Edith Wharton objected to before the First World War, and which Georgina Masson politely ignored fifty years later, but in this instance they were wrong. Italian garden planting of the nineteenth and twentieth centuries is just as worthy as that of previous ages. Certainly the power of the sun makes the pink *Rhododendron* at Villa Carlotta flower more prolifically than they do in the UK, and the desire of the Italian gardener to clip things into shape gives a certain stiffness to the scene, but it would be a pity to travel

to foreign gardens and find that they look the same as the ones at home.

When walking south from the house, the view is defined by the great groves of London plane (*Platanus* × *hispanica*) under which many ornamental shrubs thrive. This is a lovely example of the way in which Georg of Saxe-Meiningen cleverly and respectfully folded his new layers of plantsman's pleasures over the ancient terracing. Another stream forms a waterfall lined by a wall adorned with stone dwarfs. Above the house are quiet shady winding walks among the trees, perhaps the successors to those in Sommariva's English park. But the visitor will always be drawn back to the epic vista from the upper balcony, down over the parterre, out through the decorative gates and across the glittering lake to the incomparable view of the great wooded hump of the Bellagio peninsula, where the lake divides, with the Wagnerian scenery of the snow-capped mountains rising behind.

ABOVE The domed mausoleum chapel on the shore is flanked by giant plane (*Platanus*) trees. Though not accessible to the public, the chapel strikes a suitably sombre note among the pleasure-seeking everywhere around it.

OPPOSITE One of the minor pleasures of the Villa Carlotta is the long pergola hanging with *Citrus* fruit of several species and forms. This outdoor gallery of interest and beauty is glazed during the winter months.

VILLA DEL BALBIANELLO

Among all the arresting locations crowned by human improvements in this world, the site and features of the Villa del Balbianello are in the front rank. And the value is threefold: the place looks unspeakably romantic in the approach; reveals layer on layer of beauty and interest within its little world; and directs the eye outwards to framed views of such power and glory that the most ardent romantic's descriptive powers will fail. You may not have this demi-paradise to yourself, but the experience will be well worth sharing.

Balbianello is easy to find on any map. It projects into the body of Lake Como halfway along its length, swelling out from the western shore into the middle. To the approaching traveller, it looks for all the world like a substantial island, domed and covered with wood, with just the little cluster of buildings on the eastern tip visible from a distance. It has been a famously desirable destination since the end of the eighteenth century, and regularly reduces visitors to gasps of admiration.

A good deal of the fun of Balbianello is in getting there. It is possible to walk to the garden from the shore, and there will always be pleasure to be had in a walk through the woods, but this garden is intended to be reached from the lake by boat. The arrangements are simple enough. The short voyage from Lenno brings the visitor gradually round the headland, and includes views of the Villa del Balbianello's famous, triple-arched loggia and the little harbour with its saints in the act of benediction, so much admired by Georgina Masson. The passenger then steps ashore at the south-facing gates to this little paradise. Visitors have been arriving this way for a very long time: a painting of the early nineteenth century in the house shows a straw-hatted man pointing to the loggia from a boat rowed by two stout lads, while the smoke-belching *Lario*, the first pleasure steamer on the lake, approaches from Como.

The layout seen today was formed by Cardinal Angelo Maria Durini. He had failed in his attempt to purchase the nearby Isola Comacina, the only island on the lake, anciently famous as the local seat of resistance by last-ditch Romans against the barbarian hordes. The cardinal therefore turned his attention to Balbianello, which he purchased in 1785. Here he transformed the former convent into a villa for his summer use, and added the signature loggia in its present knockout position, thereby ensuring the open-mouthed gratitude of future generations.

In the nineteenth century, Balbianello became a significant seat of radical republican activity, and the Carbonari met here. The aim of this secret society of Italian intellectuals was the unification of Italy, but their plan of action was rather vague. The site's owner was himself of the nationalist persuasion, for which reason he gave one of their leaders – Silvio Pellico – the safe post of tutor to his children. In 1820, Pellico was dramatically arrested at Balbianello by the Austrian authorities, and the owner wisely decamped to Belgium. There he was supported by the wealthy Arconati

Visconti family, themselves in self-imposed exile. Visconti soon bought Balbianello himself, and the garden remained in the possession of the family until 1923. The elaborate balustrade in front of the old church bears their famous emblem of a serpent with a man in its mouth.

Just before the First World War, an American – Butler Ames – who had seen the property from the lake, besieged its last Visconti owner with ever-larger cash offers. Eventually, in 1919, he bought it. Thereafter, Balbianello became a place of

ABOVE The triple-arched loggia of the villa, strategically placed for maximum effect, is decorated in delicately extravagant style with the shoots and leaves of a single plant of the creeping fig (*Ficus pumila*).
RIGHT The arms of the Arconati Visconti family, who owned this place for many years, are represented in the balustrades. Theirs is the dramatic emblem of the serpent consuming (or ejecting?) a man.

perpetual pleasure for Ames, his wife Fifi and their endless flow of guests. This happy interregnum saw the site safely through the difficult years of the mid-twentieth century. Then, in 1954, came the beginning of the modern era, and of Balbianello as it is now seen. Ames died that year, and the site was bought by Guido Monzino, whose family had made an immense fortune as pioneer Italian department store owners. Monzino, however, was not interested in the trappings of commerce. He was a very extraordinary man, whose ideas and character permeate this place so completely that, to understand what is here, we must learn something of his personality.

ABOVE The creeping fig (*Ficus pumila*) grows here, there and everywhere across the arches and columns, distracting the disbelieving eye from the memorable lake scenery beyond the balustrade.

Most people who visit are amazed to discover that he was the leader of the first Italian expedition to reach the top of Mount Everest, and the first Italian to reach the North Pole. He was also a collector of art and decorative objects of the front rank, as anyone will confirm from a tour of the house. Monzino bought Balbianello because of its exceptional situation and for the opportunity it afforded him to mould it to his own requirements. He believed, with some justification, that, after the assassination of Aldo Moro by the Red Brigades in 1978, he was next on the list. This explains the rather James Bond-like choice of location and the outlandish system of hidden passages, some cut through the solid rock, linking the various parts of the property.

He altered the house in ways that make the modern visitor wonder what it might have been like previously. His transformation left the exterior of the buildings essentially

unchanged, and he kept at least the character of the sequence of modest-sized rooms within. Monzino was especially a fan of Georgian England, so that Chippendale furniture, campaign chests from naval ships including the *Victory*, glass paintings and grandfather clocks abound. On the walls are endless depictions of scenes on Lake Como in every medium, so that the scenery in each window appears a continuation of the collection. In glass cabinets and on chimneypieces are items from the many world cultures which fascinated him, from ancient Chinese dynasties to Mayan holy men and the France of Louis XV. In all these groupings, there is the rare combination of money, taste, expertise and a meticulous and thoroughgoing organizational flair. The museum of exploration on the top floor is a revelation in its own right. It makes me feel exhausted just thinking about it. When adapting the garden to his very particular needs, Monzino was as attentive as he had been to the house alterations. During all the urgent, widely travelled, self-endangering, endless campaign of Monzino's life, and his financing of

whole multinational expeditions, he smoked heavily, to the extent that he became debilitated with emphysema and died of its effects. Everything is maintained just as he left it, according to his precise specifications. It all seems impossibly contradictory, but here are the results of a life well lived. He was not like the rest of us.

The visitor will find that the walk up to the loggia curves gently past lawns shaven to a degree apparently at odds with the requirements of gravity. All around are bay (*Laurus*

ABOVE A priest blesses those who arrive and depart by boat. A bench overhung with *Wisteria*, trained up the flanking plane (*Platanus*) trees, awaits those overwhelmed by culture and scenery.

OPPOSITE ABOVE A painting of the 1830s depicts enthusiasts being rowed towards Balbianello. The first passenger steamer, the *Lario*, can just be seen approaching from Como.

OPPOSITE BELOW The modern arrival by boat from Lenno reveals how little has changed. Though it is possible to walk, half the pleasure lies in rounding the peninsula on the lake.

nobilis) hedges neatly clipped on the same basis, hanging over the lapping water's edge, and the elegantly mottled bark of plane (*Platanus*) trees pollarded just so, leaving the viewer to wonder just how such control is achieved by fellow human beings.

Not that all this tonsorial artistry detracts from the fairy-tale atmosphere. It only adds to it. The retaining wall by the walk is hung with classical swags of ivy (*Hedera*), and the same

---

OPPOSITE The meticulous shaving of the crown of a holm oak (*Quercus ilex*) in front of Guido Monzino's former office into a mushroom shape keeps the view clear along the lake. It is a skilled annual exercise.

BELOW LEFT The earnest pilgrim has the special privilege of the gradual approach by boat, followed by the warm greeting of the staff as they step gingerly on to the shore.

BELOW RIGHT Narrow walks criss-cross the site, each affording the desirable sensation of momentary privacy in this little Elysian Field. *Wisteria* drapes the walls along the visitor's progress.

OVERLEAF The exactness of everything seen is the key to its character. It is difficult to mow a lawn this shape so neatly; it is awkward to train the ivy (*Hedera*) to just this height and thickness; but when such jobs are done well, the result is a unique composition.

climber clothes the lower halves of the tree trunks – just as Pliny the Younger wrote in his letter describing his own garden in the first century CE.

Once on the height, the loggia's columns are covered with an elaborate reticulated pattern of creeping fig (*Ficus pumila*), all from the same root at ground level. The brain can only begin to compute the time, patience and exactness required to clip it all just so on a regular basis.

When looking down to the right from this point, the crown of a big holm oak (*Quercus ilex*) is moulded into a perfect round so that Monzino could admire the thrilling view of Bellagio parked neatly on top of it while seated at his Chippendale partners' desk. And in case the visitor imagines they can break free of his oversight now that he is no longer with them, think again, and look down into the interior of the ice house, where his tomb resides, ever watchful.

As the garden is small, it can occupy the exploring visitor for only a short time. Its pleasure lies in its deliciously precise combination of green overlays of turf, box (*Buxus*) and bay (*Laurus nobilis*) and the welcome shade of meticulously

shaped trees. There is sufficient sculpture to keep the eye entertained, all of good quality. Among the best is Monzino's coat of arms over the entrance to the house, depicting a goat on a mountain peak, with his motto 'Gradatim scenditur ad altem' [Step by step we climb to the top].

The Fondo per l'Ambiente Italiano (FAI) are now charged with guarding the flame of Guido Monzino's zeal. He was a demanding taskmaster, a stickler for correctness in all things, and also a man with the single-minded energy and skills to make all this work. We should be grateful for such a man at such a place.

The abiding impression of Balbianello will always be that loggia. The best view is north along to the lake towards Bellagio and the towering, snow-capped peaks beyond it, some clothed with sweet chestnut (*Castanea sativa*), others bare rock, nearly all sweeping straight down into the lake

OPPOSITE ABOVE Classical statues, ivy (*Hedera*)-clad trees and big pots of *Hydrangea* combine to set up rhythms of orderly beauty along the walks at Balbianello.

OPPOSITE BELOW Precision and romance are not instinctive bedfellows, but Guido Monzino saw that the combination of neatly pollarded trees, accurately dished slopes of turf and box (*Buxus*) edging of architectural regularity were the ideal foreground to natural grandeur.

ABOVE The gardens of Villa del Balbianello are full of thoughtful contrasts, as here between the order of architectural terracing and the disorder of the natural outcrop. This balance between control and freedom is carefully maintained.

VILLA
SOMMI PICENARDI

ISTE TERRARUM NOBIS PRAETER OMNES ANGULIS RIDET
(Inscription on the south front of the house. For
the translation, read on.)

The stretch of countryside known as the Brianza, to
the south of Lake Como, is largely untroubled by the
arrival of crowds of visitors. It is a region of wooded
hills, full of birdsong in the spring, with the broad River Adda,
which steadily empties into Lake Como, flowing quietly by.
Stendhal famously admired it for 'the coolness of the woods,
the verdure of the meadows, the murmur of the waters'. In
the unremarkable towns and villages of the Brianza, everyday
life goes on. One of these villages is Olgiate Molgora, a few
kilometres south of the industrial town of Lecco, on the
south-eastern corner of the lake, and not far west of famously
picturesque Bergamo, perched on its hill.

I arrived one spring morning at the surprisingly important-
looking village railway station (Italy still has such things,
with regular services and affordable fares) and began the
pleasant walk up a gentle hill to the Villa Sommi Picenardi on
the outskirts of the village. It is a good way to arrive at this
garden, with its rural setting gradually unfolding all around.
On this particular morning, three cuckoos were singing from
different directions and at varying distances.

Soon I came to a significant point in my journey, where
the winding lane straightened into a broad avenue, whose
flanking gate piers announced it as the Viale Sommi
Picenardi. Nearby stand the village war memorial and two

OPPOSITE Sculpture, fountains, panels of turf and neat hedges set the tone
in the terrace garden at the Villa Sommi Picenardi, where all is seemly
order on a pleasingly modest scale.

civic buildings, the library and the primary school, dedicated
to illustrious members of the Sommi Picenardi family. The
tone set, I walked more thoughtfully along the avenue of
columnar oaks (*Quercus robur* Fastigiata Group) rhythmically
set above a hornbeam (*Carpinus betulus*) hedge. Dead ahead
I could see straight into the park of my destination, where a
curly, wrought-iron grille revealed a big yellow house at the
top of an open lawn.

The garden as seen from this point is a creation of around
1880, when the then owners decided to change the sloping
agricultural fields south of the house into an English
garden. This had an informal open lawn scattered with
clumps and specimens of ornamental trees, through which
a new carriage drive wound circuitously up the slope to
right and left to extend the visitor experience and show
the new layout to advantage. The remains of this drive,
cambered in the nineteenth-century manner to shed water
efficiently, are still clearly visible in the grass. The trees
are now noble specimens, conveying an effect of calm
splendour everywhere. What the visitor does not expect is
hidden behind the house. It is a big surprise, and well worth
the wait.

The Sommi Picenardi came here in 1910, when they
bought the property from the Sala family, who had, in the
traditional way, come here for the summer months from
their town house in Milan for the previous two centuries.
Azzurra Sommi Picenardi and her sister are now the fourth
generation here, and they divide the work of opening the
garden and organizing the inevitable weddings between
them. They do this with uncommon skill. Everything that
the enthusiast could wish to see is here, but the dead hand
of corporate entertainment has never touched this place.

Refreshments are there of course by arrangement, but this is a private house, so expect no retail fripperies. You are a guest here, not a customer. Long may it remain so.

Like many estates across Europe, the house made its first appearance in the historical record as a defensive watchtower – in this instance, in the fifteenth century. A century later, a farmhouse was built, with no pretensions to luxury. It was a tenant farm belonging to the Vimercati family. It is not difficult to imagine its land running down the southerly slope towards the site of the present railway line.

In the seventeenth century, the Vimercati sold the property to the Sala of Milan. Nothing much happened at first, as the new owners did not visit, but as time went on they gradually began to take an interest in the site as a potential destination for *villeggiatura*. The word *villeggiatura* seems to preoccupy the minds of academics considerably, but in modern Italian it simply means 'a holiday'. A spell of *villeggiatura* in the summer months implies getting away from it all, indulging oneself in rural pastimes, reading, gardening, spending time with like-minded friends and generally pottering about – in a word, recreation.

The farmhouse was accordingly remodelled into a villa, playing down its functional character in favour of polite decoration. By the end of the seventeenth century, when the work was done, this exercise required the presence of a rectangular courtyard in front of the villa. A tall front wall was built to form this courtyard of honour. The villa itself was considerably aggrandized, assuming more or less its present appearance, though the courtyard wall was later taken down. Now there is a long regular building stuccoed in yellow, with wings breaking forward squarely at either end. Along the top of this south front is a Latin inscription notifying all cultivated onlookers that 'this corner of the earth smiles more for us than any other'. Appropriately, it is a slightly reworked quotation from Horace – a ready source of suitable phrases celebrating the joys of patrician rural life.

RIGHT Stone swags and vases on the staircase of the Italian garden lead the eye down to the parterre.

OPPOSITE ABOVE The broad lawn of the English garden stretches towards the entrance front of the villa. On the right is the crown of the great plane (*Platanus*) tree, with chairs set out in its refreshing shade.

OPPOSITE RIGHT The elegant 'modern' parterre, framed in hornbeam (*Carpinus betulus*) tunnels, is a worthy addition to the garden at the Villa Sommi Picenardi. The box (*Buxus*) looks a little poorly from moth damage, but it is on the mend.

The work on the villa seems to have been completed in 1702, as that is the date of the dedication of the chapel in the western wing. The chapel is a worthy destination in its own right, being full of minor pleasures such as a framed papal indulgence dated 1770, long after such practices were supposed to have been swept away. Quite what the garden looked like in 1702 is not known, but another generation introduced something priceless.

Walking round the villa to see what is at the back is a compulsory activity at the Villa Sommi Picenardi. No greater contrast with the languid expansiveness of the English

LEFT A wing of the house looks on as the central staircase zigzags up the terraces to the line of sober statues on the second level.

ABOVE A boy rides on a dolphin in a grotto-like niche decorated in the most delicate fashion with shells, both carved and real.

garden on the south front can be imagined than what is found here. A terraced garden of superlative regular neatness rises up from a turf parterre, the whole performance carefully highlighted with tellingly placed mosaics, statues, delicate fountains and shellwork. The more the eye dwells on this precious survival, the better it gets, but perhaps the real wonder is that it is here at all.

This garden seems to have been the final act of the baroque redevelopment of the layout, and to have been created in about 1730. That date suggests a later hand than the work on the villa. The taste, however, is conservative, so perhaps this is the final act of an old maestro. We will probably never have the answers to these questions. We do know, however, that this part of the garden became known as the 'little Versailles of the Brianza'. How proud the makers must have been of that: it still brings a smile to the faces of the present owners. A big part of the charm of this garden to a modern eye is its apparently modest scale – all things being relative. There

seems no trace here of the shock and awe beloved of the baroque mind, whose first intention is to render the grandest visitor momentarily speechless with the overwhelming power and glory of the achievement. There is no knockout blow here: no avenue marching off into eternity; no thundering cascade; and no heroic parade of statuary on a theme of haughty classical divinities. This is that unheard-of thing – the low-key baroque. The Sun King would have been nonplussed.

OPPOSITE ABOVE The trunk of the master plane (*Platanus*) tree in front of the house is vast, as if from some fairy tale. Its great plates of mottled brown bark are covered lower down with velvety green moss.

OPPOSITE BELOW The crown of the great plane frames a statue in a magnificent baroque arched niche set into the wall of the house.

BELOW A statue in a grove of trees sums up the character of the English garden at the Villa Sommi Picenardi: the more you look, the more you will see.

Perhaps part of the reason may be that, by 1730, the rococo influence was growing everywhere, leaving less room for swagger and more for intimacy. Nonetheless, there are few rococo twirls here, and certainly none of the expected asymmetry, so we must simply accept that the result of fitting the proportions of the garden into the combination of the width of the villa and the rise of the slope is this very charming set piece.

There is one more pleasant puzzle to be taken into account. This garden seems to have been altered around 1920 by the present family. No one is quite sure what was done, but it has been suggested that, while the framework is early eighteenth century, some of the decorative overlay may be early twentieth century. This might, for example, include the parterre at the foot of the terraces. This is laid out as neat sections of turf interlaced with grey gravel paths and a pattern of circular pools, with some simple topiary regularly positioned.

The effect is quite different to the arabesques of box (*Buxus*) that are expected in such a plan. Both these styles are illustrated in Dézallier d'Argenville's *Theory and Practice of Gardening* (1709), the standard work for would-be emulators of Louis XIV's style. Those box scrolls feature in the *parterre de broderie* [embroidered garden]; the patterns of turf against gravel are called *parterre à l'anglaise* [English garden], simply because of the use of green turf. The English themselves termed this style 'cutwork'. There is a magnificent modern recreation of it in the orangery garden at Versailles itself. The effect on the mind is of a pleasing counterbalance between the rigour of the pattern and the relative simplicity of the green lawns. Here, the pleasure is heightened by the tinkling refinement of the slender jets of water rising from the pools. All the rules are acknowledged and mastered, but applied without a heavy hand.

The mosaic work on the central baroque staircase is worth a good look, and is in such good condition that I wonder whether it may not be part of the twentieth-century changes. It represents generic twirling shoots, and is finely wrought in

RIGHT Two styles alongside one another. The hedge-framed seat, perhaps more for looking at than sitting on, is set against a loose grove of trees on an open lawn.

OVERLEAF The owner's eye view of the terraced garden sees it rising boldly and regularly like a standing ovation. Delusions of grandeur are kept in check by the simple palette of greens.

pale shades of pink and grey. Similarly, the niche on the half-landing, a focal point of the whole layout, is full of interest for the lover of detail, with shells pressed by some hand of the past into damp lime mortar, including a rim of scallop shells around the edge of the arch. This makes the mind wonder how so slight a fabric can survive the rough and tumble of the ages. We must be grateful for such miracles. The staircase itself – the focal point of the whole enterprise – makes a zigzag pattern as it rises, and its balustrades are entertainingly formed of stone carved into many swags. After climbing the staircase, the visitor reaches a terrace covered simply in a lawn, like a bowling alley, with a tall box (*Buxus*) hedge disguising the wall at the back. On this terrace, and overlooking it from above, arranged in a careful display, are statues of classical gods on their pedestals. They are not apparently in any particular order of significance, and

again neither large nor demonstrative, so that their presence represents seemly order rather than a big allegorical message. The pattern on the ground makes more sense from up here – as it should – and the garden engages in a conversation with the façade of the villa. The theatrical quality is unmistakable. This must be the ideal setting for *Don Giovanni* if the orchestra could be fitted in somewhere.

At the western end of the villa is a decorative garden laid out around 1930 in the manner of a rococo parterre. It is lovely and delicate in its refined colours and textures, and cleverly placed here in order not to clash with the big set pieces on either front. From the intended viewpoint, a

BELOW The pattern of features comes to life as the visitor moves around the garden. Here, the theatrical quality is reinforced by the play of light and shade on the surfaces and fountains.

box (*Buxus*) parterre opens out around a little lawn in the foreground, then closes back in to form an elaborately flowing pattern. This is all the more enjoyable to the eye for being skilfully placed on a slightly dished slope, which gradually rises away from the eye, making it readily readable. The parterre is framed in a hornbeam (*Carpinus betulus*) tunnel with doors and windows cut in at intervals, forming a perfect atmosphere of intimacy, a complete garden in itself. It makes an ideal *giardino segreto* [private garden for family and friends]. For many years they have referred to it as the *labirinto* [maze], but it can never have been intended as one of those. As a piece of historical revivalism, it is completely

ABOVE LEFT A rather effete-looking Neptune might command a pond, but not the ocean. His place in the general scheme of things is more important than his individual presence.

ABOVE RIGHT Decorative mosaic work of a refined order and lasting beauty is set into a terrace wall. It shows how to represent twining shoots and flowers using little squares of coloured stone.

convincing, with no sense of pastiche. In style, it very much resembles the garden made for Mary (of William and Mary) at the palace of Het Loo in the Netherlands in the 1680s, recreated two centuries later.

Returning to the English garden on the south front, there are many things to admire here too, in addition to the ornamental trees on that grass slope. The planter did his work well, since everywhere the visitor looks the trees are skilfully placed, controlling the view. This is always tricky to achieve, since the first effect comes from the eighteenth-century 'Capability' Brown idea of trees as scenery in various shades of green, while the second effect derives from the nineteenth century desire to form collections of ideal specimens with dramatic variety of form and colour. The later approach wishes each tree to stand free of its neighbour so that its branches can sweep down to the ground, and to be seen as a prize item in a living catalogue. Both these intentions are successfully achieved at Villa Sommi Picenardi. Looking down from the villa, ideal specimens of big cedars

(*Cedrus*) and beeches (*Fagus*) punctuate the scene. The champion tree of all is the enormous London plane (*Platanus × hispanica*) in front of the house. It was planted in 1810 as one of a pair. Its counterpart never thrived from the beginning, and with the passage of time the discrepancy became more and more unsatisfactory, so the runt was cut down. The survivor is of immense dimensions. Its present height is around 30 metres/100 feet, which is to say seriously tall, but not exceptional. Its crown has a spread of an astonishing 46 metres/150 feet, which makes it a magnificent shady bower for the warmer months, of which there are many here. But the real test of any monster tree is its girth at breast height, which in this instance is 9.3 metres/31 feet. These are pointless statistics without some kind of comparison, but for anyone wondering just how big this tree is I recommend the usual test of simply walking up to the trunk and being overwhelmed by its colossal size. If it were merely huge, that might be informative, but there is more to it than this. Like all planes, it is blessed with the singular beauty of its bark, in great irregular plates of varying shades of light brown, and all this is overlaid with a wonderful layer of dark green furry moss, which makes the laying on of hands impossible to resist. When seen from a distance, the whole tree is magnificently regular in form, and its memorably paternal character is skilfully reinforced by the placement of a semicircle of comfortable chairs under its far-spreading crown, as if the tree were about to tell us all a story. No one will pretend that the Villa Sommi Picenardi is one of the great gardens of Europe, or perhaps even of Italy, but as an unspoilt example of a quietly placed villa with an unfolding story of successive styles, richly imbued with the personal tastes and whims of the many generations who have lived here, it is irresistible. Its continuing story in the hands of the present owners, with the next generation coming along nicely, will be well worth following.

RIGHT An oblique view from the house over the Italian garden. Those who are resistant to the charms of the formal garden might well feel their position becoming undermined in this lovely place.

VILLA SERBELLONI

O n Lake Como, everything is secondary to the view. All responses are determined by the feelings of enclosure imposed by the steep wooded banks rising to towering peaks all around, so that the various entertainments offered by the villages and gardens along the shore are tiny details seen against the dramatic backdrop. A glance at the map, however, soon raises curiosity about the different branches and basins of the lake, and whether they are more or less the same as the one in view, or different in appearance and atmosphere. One relatively short way of answering these questions is to take a walk through the grounds of the Villa Serbelloni at Bellagio.

From whichever direction the centre of the lake is approached, the wooded hump above Bellagio is a striking object. On the map, it is the tip of the promontory forming the crotch at which the two legs join. The water flowing south from the Alps splits evenly from here towards Como in the south-western corner and Lecco in the south-east, where it drains into the winding River Adda. The same happens to the wind, which blows steadily from the north each morning, so that the local name for the tip of the peninsula is the Punta Spartivento [point where the wind divides]. It seems likely from the map that, if the visitor could stand on top of the hump, this would be the only place on the lake from which they could see all three branches of the lake. This is indeed the case, and the best reason for walking through these gardens.

The grounds of the Villa Serbelloni have always been in private ownership, but there is a long tradition of controlled public access through them. This continues today under the present owners – the Rockefeller Foundation of New York – who on a regular basis delegate the leadership of tours to the local authority. From the town square by the church, where the tour begins, the approach looks impossibly steep, but the walk follows the carriage drive in its zigzag course to come to the top without the need for anything more serious than a desire to view memorable scenery.

The strategic significance of the site is immediately obvious: from the top anyone would readily be able to see trouble coming from a long distance, especially from the north – the most likely source. Of the golden-age Roman Pliny the Younger's two villas on the lake, one seems likely to have stood on this headland. Could it have been the site of the present castle ruins on top of the hill? Commanding view, certainly, but exposed to storms from all directions. Perhaps the site of the present villa itself is more likely, with its monumental prospect of two branches of the lake from a position some way below the wooded peak, and comfortably facing south over terraced gardens.

Walking up through the grounds, the first impression is of the gradual unfolding of glorious views over the surroundings. The handsome Romanesque church of San Giacomo in the middle of Bellagio is seen from above, as if the visitor were in flight. How often do people look down on such a building? The roof covering of slates – like the uneven scales of a fish – is memorable, and so are the three round apses of the east end, directly below. Behind it stretches the roofline of the town itself, with the lake surface gleaming beyond.

OPPOSITE The real reason for visiting the grounds of the Villa Serbelloni is to enjoy the epic views out over the three branches of the lake. Here, pines and ornamental conifers are the foreground to a vista over the Como branch, with the ferry approaching Bellagio.

The character of the grounds at the Villa Serbelloni is of a woodland garden of ornamental trees: walnuts (*Juglans*), cedars (*Cedrus*), *Magnolia*, yews (*Taxus*) and hemlocks (*Tsuga*). These offer welcome shade and variety, but nothing much to excite the plant-lover. Much more to that taste is the chance display of wild flowers, which are everywhere. The lawns are covered in thyme and bugle (*Ajuga*), and in the spring there are early spider orchids (*Ophrys sphegodes*) to be spotted by the sharp-eyed. Banks of primroses (*Primula vulgaris*) and violets tumble down towards the rugged retaining walls and jutting crags, which themselves are home to hellebores and *Cyclamen*. Although the 'hallowed Sfondrati woods' beloved of Stendhal, who came here in 1825, are now modern plantations, the ancient ground flora remains, so the visitor can admire, for example, butcher's broom (*Ruscus aculeatus*) everywhere and marvel that a plant in the lily family could be so tough and prickly.

Scattered here and there are garden buildings of one sort or another: some are built as barns, while others form elegant additions to the garden scene, from which no doubt marvellous views are obtained. The visitor on the tour will never know this for sure, because these little buildings are all in use by the visiting academics who come here by invitation for conferences and seminars for a few weeks at a time. It has been suggested that some academics come here to complete their doctoral theses, but that seems unlikely. One glance out of the window would put an end to that notion, and how could you not look?

The academics have been coming here since 1959, when the previous owner, Ella Walker, died, and left the Villa Serbelloni to the Rockefeller Foundation with all sorts of conditions and caveats regarding the future use of the buildings and grounds. She had bought the estate out of hotel ownership in 1930, using family money derived from the Canadian Club whisky brand, and she made it her business to put personal wealth and influence to charitable uses in this rather special location.

Soon the visitor comes to a long perspective down the Como branch of the lake, typically glittering far below, with uncertain clouds hanging on the framing mountains. The familiar wooded headland of the Dosso di Lavedo can be seen, with the buildings of the Villa del Balbianello on its

---

BELOW The distinctive shape of the Villa Serbelloni estate, which forms the startling wooded hump above the town of Bellagio, is best appreciated from the lake.
OPPOSITE ABOVE A service building lines the drive, leading the eye south past cypresses (*Cupressus sempervirens*) to the mountains beyond.

tip. Along the intervening shore, the scattered villas of the nineteenth-century Milanese patricians mingle with the woods and open spaces.

The Villa Serbelloni is then glimpsed through a mixed planting of Japanese maples (*Acer palmatum*), but it is even better to look instead out over the descending terraces below. This is a big panorama, the land falling through olives and cypresses (*Cupressus*), with the former Capuchin convent prominent. The former Anglican church, from the days when the British writ ran here before 1914, has now been converted

---

LEFT Pines and cypresses (*Cupressus sempervirens*) frame the long view down through the Tuscan garden. In the centre of the picture is the Villa Gotica, once the Anglican church.

OVERLEAF The roofs of the various villages which make up the town of Bellagio are scattered over the hills and mountains to the south, along the Como branch of the lake.

into the Villa Gotica. Just beyond it is the Villa Giulia, once the property of Leopold I of Belgium, Prince Albert's uncle. He blasted through solid rock to level an avenue and obtain views of two branches of the lake from his windows. Past that point, the ground begins to rise steeply into the mountains, with the highest point of Monte San Primo in the middle of a long ridge on the horizon.

A little further along the route the visitor comes to a noble view over the Lecco branch of the lake. The comparison is striking. The Como branch is rather shiny, and cheerfully populated with villas, hotels and the other impedimenta of a leisured life, with passenger boats constantly plying from shore to shore, but the Lecco branch is utterly different. It is dark, severe, craggy and a little intimidating, with hardly a boat to be seen except the occasional fisherman lying off the pretty lakeshore village of Pescallo, a favourite corner for escapist romantics. The route then proceeds through lovely groves of mixed trees and shrubs, looking down over the *Wisteria* and *Camellia* around the villa, towards the summit. On the way is a statue bearing the name of Pliny, but that

identity can be safely dismissed, since the figure has the flowing curly beard of a biblical saint.

As the walk continues to climb, the feeling of altitude is impressively reinforced by the sight of flocks of red kites below, pushing against the breeze.

It is something of a surprise to enter the long grotto, cut through the rock with a kink in the middle to create a momentary sense of romantic unease in the gloom. At one end, the entrance frames a lovely view of Varenna on the far side of the lake, beneath its little castle.

Once on the top, the visitor stands among the castle ruins. These are more extensive than might be expected, and include a long grey curtain wall on a vaguely octagonal plan and the obvious remains of a chapel with its half-round apse. They would appear more evocative if the space inside

BELOW On some spring days, the haze on Lake Como clears. This is the moment to sit on this elegant bench among the castle ruins on the top of the promontory at the Villa Serbelloni and gaze along the lake to the snow-covered mountains closing the vista to the north.

them were not neatly mown with a silly little flower bed in the middle. If the wild flowers were allowed to grow more freely . . . but the visitor can stop worrying about all that, because the big attraction here is the view. For the first time, at this point the northern branch of the lake is seen in all its glory, and the big eye-catcher is the magnificent wall of the Swiss Alps closing the panorama at the end of the lake. The weather on Lake Como is typically hazy, as if a muslin veil were suspended in front of the mountains, but occasionally the light is crystal clear. Then everyone gasps at the grandeur of the scene, especially when, in spring, the great peaks are covering with gleaming snow a third of the way down. Below, the rock outcrops, scattered trees, tufts of rough grass

and shrubs give some idea of what it might have been like here before the refining hand of humans began to smooth things over. In all, this is the character of the grounds of the Villa Serbelloni: a mingling of the wild and the cultivated, with the former always ready to reassert its authority. Perhaps that might not be such a bad thing.

ABOVE The view south-west from the upper part of the garden looks along the Como branch. The doubtful haze which hangs in the atmosphere is characteristic of the lake.

VILLA CIPRESSI AND
VILLA MONASTERO

Varenna is a lovely spot. The village stands quite on its own on the eastern lake shore, piled up into a picturesque heap of apricot and terracotta, with the church spire neatly placed on top to complete the painterly composition. Above it all rises the grey and green sobriety of the natural mountain flank, with the romantic tower of the Castello di Vezio keeping watch.

The apparent isolation is an illusion. The ferries ply frequently here, across to Menaggio and Bellagio; the road from Lecco to the Alps skirts the town; and a very useful train station with regular services brings holidaymakers up from Milan – an hour to the south. Amazingly, this stretch of line was the world's first electric railway, completed at the beginning of the twentieth century.

This happy combination of a beautiful setting and convenient access has naturally brought many pleasure-seekers to Varenna over the years. In the golden years either side of 1900, when the modern face of such places was formed, the villas scattered through the town were populated in due season by the visiting bourgeoisie. The terraces and passenger boats were thus the resort of public figures and captains of industry. The homburg, the cigar and the waxed moustache were everywhere. Hotel lobbies maintained daily lists of distinguished people gracing the town with their presence.

Among the many charms of modern Varenna is the welcome fact that two of these villas – the Villa Cipressi and the Villa

Monastero – readily open their gardens to the visiting public. They form a long coda to the outline of the town when seen from the lake, stretching out along the shore to form its southern boundary. Villa Cipressi is the more obvious at first, sitting up at the level of the road, richly coloured and immediately eye-catching. Villa Monastero is next door, but the house is quite different and less conspicuous. It has a long front of pale grey arcades in line with its gardens, and is relatively low along the lake edge. The two sites overlap each other in a surprising way, as the boathouse of one stands in front of the garden of the other, but neither is compromised, and perhaps both may be said to gain from the arrangement. Though these have always been, and still are today, quite separate establishments, there is a strong feeling in my mind that they are intimately related, so that they seem like non-identical twins. I wonder how they feel about this comparison.

Stepping into the Villa Cipressi today, through its discreetly sliding glass doors, is an interesting experience. There is a moment of uncertainty as to whether the visitor should be there at all, as this has been for many years a particular kind of study centre with all facilities. It was the first place I ever stayed when I came to Lake Como many years ago. Standing in the hall, there is an audible bustle and chatter of activity from invisible rooms a few metres away. Overhead are decorative ceilings of high quality. If this brief experience is intended to make visitors want to stay longer, it is successful.

Close at hand is the reception desk, at which a quietly professional lady produces garden tickets in exchange for a nominal payment, and indicates the little side door through I should make my exit. Once the door had shut, I was in a little

OPPOSITE Oleander (*Nerium*) flowers colour the view from the barley-twist column in front of the Villa Monastero to the skilfully placed Villa Cipressi, standing among the trees from which it takes its name.

courtyard formed by the rooms of the villa. From here, the
gravel walks begin to meander down towards the lake shore,
flanked with lawns and the specimen shrubs favoured by the
international set of Edwardian Europe: the Chusan palm
(*Trachycarpus fortunei*); *Rosa banksiae* 'Lutea' with its curtains
of tiny primrose buttonhole flowers; various forms of *Yucca*
and *Agave*; and a certain amount of seasonal bedding. It all
feels rather like some of the older properties on the French
Riviera. The standard of maintenance has more to do with
holding the fort than winning the show, but all is neat and
seemly. Nothing could compete with the backdrop of natural
scenery, anyway.

The two most enjoyable features in the garden of the Villa
Cipressi are the wall of *Wisteria* and the pergola terrace in
front of the house. *Wisteria* very much enjoys the conditions
on Lake Como. The northern European cannot help but
be overwhelmed by its performance in mid-spring, when
it flowers in such profusion as to stop visitors in their

tracks. If the physical beauty of its casually lax, amethyst-
coloured blooms were not enough, the scent would do
the job on its own. Its richness drifts on the air, causing
gasps of disbelief from passers-by. Here at the Villa Cipressi
Wisteria covers a 6-metre/20-foot retaining wall for a length
of 90 metres/295 feet, and is correctly pruned, so that the
wall above the path is entirely covered in its flowers. It is a
memorable scene.

The pergola in front of the house, overlooking the lake, is
typical of those erected by foreigners from the grey north
when they arrived at Lake Como. It does its job here well as

OPPOSITE The cool grey block of the Villa Monastero stretches out low
against the shoreline of Varenna. Its arcaded façade overlooks varied
groups of garden columns and pavilions.

ABOVE The long terraces of the Villa Monastero sweep down to the shore
of Lake Como. The eye is led north along the lake to the mountains
which close the vista.

an evocative garden feature, cleverly focusing the eye on the framed headland at Bellagio, dead ahead. There can be no lovelier place to eat your breakfast than on the terrace, with the morning sun pushing its golden streak along the surface of the lake.

Moving next door to the Villa Monastero, there is an inevitable expectation that things will be exactly the same, only different. In fact, though there are many resemblances, the Villa Monastero's character is quite distinct. The villa has a long history, beginning, as the name suggests, as a convent and remade as a country house in the seventeenth century. The prevailing hand in what is seen now is that of Walter Kees, a Leipzig entrepreneur, who made this his holiday home between 1897 and 1909. The extent of his ambition is immediately apparent on looking into the house, which, like the garden, is thoughtfully managed by the local authority. A great imperial staircase is adorned with startling pictorial panels of four great Germans – J.S. Bach, Immanuel Kant,

the sculptor Andreas Schlüter and the physicist Hermann von Helmholtz. This distinctive group of characters from various periods and fields of endeavour reflects Kees's personal enthusiasms, rather than being just four more of the usual choices. And do not miss the sensational sunken bath on the first floor!

The garden is laid out over upper and lower terraces, with important-looking additions from Kees's period. These include a semicircular temple looking out over the lake. It is perfectly fine in every way except that the architect understood neither classical architecture nor the practicalities of admiring a view, since one of the columns is placed directly in the middle. Other columns appear in front of the

ABOVE The Villa Cipressi, viewed from the garden of the Villa Monastero, sits up high above its *Wisteria*-draped terraces. In the foreground is its eye-catchingly stripy boathouse.

house as the architect worked his way through his repertoire of styles, including some delicious baroque-revival, barley-twist versions. These are free-standing, but may perhaps once have supported a pergola, as at the Villa Cipressi. The open temple over the lake also makes the most of the view next door, so that the Villa Cipressi, framed in the trees from which it takes its name, appears as a sort of ideal pavilion, close enough to evoke admiration but not so close as to suggest intrusion.

The lower terrace at the Villa Monastero continues southward for a considerable distance. It must indeed have been a marvellous place in its party heyday before all that came to an end in 1914. One of the best surviving features is the long border of *Citrus* trees just south of the house. These are drawn up in ideal fashion: evenly spaced; neatly pruned as standards; and each labelled. Everything suggests the final fulfilment of a long held wish to cultivate all the famous forms of history. Here are bergamot oranges (*Citrus × limon* Bergamot Group), grapefruit (*C. × aurantium* Grapefruit Group), kumquat (*C. japonica*) and many others, all ready be studied, gazed on, inhaled and eaten.

I am quite sure Walter Kees spent many hours of delight here among his horticultural treasures. It is a happy image of the sunny South, a haven of delight for the man from the other side of the Alps. This is the key to understanding why these places were made.

BELOW The *Citrus* collection in the garden of the Villa Monastero is an enthusiast's delight. The trees include sweet oranges (*C. sinensis*), lemons (*C. × limon*), kumquats (*C. japonica*), bergamot oranges (*C. × limon* Bergamot Group) and citrons (*C. medica*).

VILLA D'ESTE

The Villa D'Este at Cernobbio, in the southern basin of the lake not far north of the city of Como, is one of the more splendid hotel establishments along the lake shore. Its pontoon swimming pools project into the lake, visible for kilometres around, and a general air of the old-world grand hotel emanates from the villa, behind which greenery rises to the mountains. Long-serving staff in handsome uniforms greet the visitor at the gate lodge or landing stage. This is a little world of its own.

At first sight, the great house appears to be set in the typical English-style gardens of the nineteenth century, in which sinuous gravel walks cross expansive velvety lawns under big ornamental trees. If that were so, we might nod politely and continue on our way. However, there is something very special here, which makes a detour well worthwhile.

The first villa was built in 1568 to the design of Pellegrino Pellegrini for Cardinal Tolomeo Gallio of Como. It was originally the Villa Garovo, named after the mountain stream that flows through its grounds into the lake. Though many things have changed over the centuries, the double cascade and nymphaeum from that period still exists, apparently intact.

The house got its present name when the property was bought in 1815 by Caroline of Brunswick-Wolfenbüttel, whose reputation went before her across Europe. She was married to the British Prince Regent, later to succeed as King George IV. He, wanting nothing to do with her, foolishly enjoined her to travel about at her leisure. She needed no encouragement, and her increasingly splendid lifestyle wherever she went did nothing but cement her husband's reputation as, to put it mildly, an unsatisfactory husband and a pariah of public relations. Caroline's social calendar here made her a journalist's dream.

It was Caroline's idea to rename the house the Villa D'Este – a choice that has led to endless protracted explanations ever since. This property has nothing to do with the famous Villa D'Este at Tivoli, near Rome. Caroline was aware that her family descended from one Guelfo D'Este, and invoked this unsuspecting ancestor for the name of her new home. This gave it a certain *éclat* as it suggested ancient dynasties and an immemorial connection with the local soil. It is a boldly theatrical approach to history. I could amuse and shock you for pages with the anecdotes of the Princess of Wales's antics here, but we must get on.

Earlier history is evident in the precious fragment of the sixteenth-century garden, located a few metres to the north-west of the house. The first shock on reaching it is that everything is in such beautiful condition: it is as if the rest of the world has moved on in the normal way, but this little strip of sloping ground is somehow isolated from the tide of events, and has remained forever just as it was on the day it was completed. I find it impossible to look at it without my mind conjuring up the rest of the layout, which presumably once spread out from it in all directions in a similar vein. But we must be grateful for small mercies.

Standing at the foot of the layout, most of which is only a few metres wide, the visitor looks up through a sequence of features. At their feet is a bright green lawn trimmed with flower beds. Examining illustrations from the past suggests that this has always been some sort of parterre, and that the current appearance is happily appropriate.

The foot of the slope is the ideal spot to have a good look at the screen walls flanking the entrance to the nymphaeum. These run out for a considerable distance, in orderly blocks and curves, and provide a memorable introduction to the mosaic-and-stucco world within. The neat geometry of regular patterns in pleasingly pale stonework speaks of that admiration for the classical world which the sculptors were seeking to bring back to life. There is a regular rhythm of niches, each headed with a dripping fringe of tufa, to prevent the walls looking too much as if they had merely sprung from the drawing board. The blocks framing the entrance to the nymphaeum are capped with elegant segmental pediments, with pairs of stubby obelisks on top as if they were horns. The length and height of the walls also has the effect of concentrating the sightline on the view up the green lawn between the two slender cascades to the open temple of Hercules at the top.

On stepping into the partially enclosed space of the nymphaeum itself, the visitor experiences a quite new sensation. It is essentially a roofless room with straight sides and semicircular ends, which seems to have slid apart in the centre to give the view from below up to the temple. The exposed central space is filled with an elliptical pool full of mountain stream water, gently teased up here and there into delicate jets. The whole pool is framed in a beautiful wrought iron rail, wound round itself into decorative iron ropes and painted black. As so often with this style period,

---

BELOW The view up to the little Shepherd's Gate is a charming minor incident in the garden, leading the eye past ingenious planting that combines green architecture with pretty seasonal bedding.

OPPOSITE ABOVE The screen walls flanking the view up to the cascade are things of beauty in their own right. Their architectural rhythms and meticulous detailing breathe the true spirit of Mannerism.

which can reasonably be called late Renaissance spilling gradually over into Mannerism, it really pays to examine everything in detail. It is tempting to assume that the iron ropework is early nineteenth century, of the time of Princess Caroline, as that was the golden age of this fabric. If this is true, it is a very worthy addition.

The mosaic walls fold around us, populated with male figures in the form of atlantes holding the structure on their heads, upon which Ionic capitals balance. Each face is quite individual. The mosaic work is wonderfully rich and varied: there is so much to admire it is hard to know when to stop. The colours are equally fabulous, and include rich blacks and terracottas, with many patterns taken from nature, since this is a garden. Between these panels are very subtle whitish scenes from the classical world, perhaps Ovid's *Metamorphoses*, carved or cast (is it stone or stucco?) in shallow relief, so that there is a great deal of pleasure in admiring the craftsman's hand by looking across the rise and fall of the material rather than square on. The whole

pattern reminds me of an Elizabethan oak overmantel panel in a prodigy house of the 1580s, such as Levens Hall, in the English Lake District. The big difference is that, here, Italians were using these motifs with confidence and understanding, whereas in England master builders were still at the stage of copying individual features from pattern books, without any real understanding of the underlying ideas.

Standing in this special little space, it gradually dawned on me that something was missing: the element of fun. Surely once there were *giochi d'acqua* [water games] here, water-spouts waiting, at a given signal from the owner to the gardener, to shoot up from the pavement and down from the top of the wall. It sounds like something you might inflict on your worst enemy, but the gentlemen and ladies of the day half expected some such diverting squirts from unpredictable places to cool them down and relieve some of the stuffiness of the reception. Anyone who recalls what it was like it was as a child to run through a lawn sprinkler on a summer afternoon will have some idea of just how much fun this can be.

From the nymphaeum the visitor looks up the slope to the double cascade, lined by an avenue of tall, richly green cypresses (*Cupressus sempervirens*), which maintain the

LEFT At the top of the green lawn, flanked by the long arms of the cascade, the visitor finds Hercules despatching another overconfident opponent. Behind them, the mountain stream flows into the grotto-like temple to power the cascades.

ABOVE The low pressure of the mountain stream ensures that the water in the two granite arms of the cascade comes gently plashing down the tray-like steps, generating a restful and refreshing atmosphere.

seclusion of this garden from its surroundings. From time to time, this vision is momentarily interrupted by a passing car on its way to a hotel car park, preventing the visitor getting too carried away with the romance of the past.

The cascades are narrow, and flow down either side of a green lawn, a sort of *tapis vert*. The water pressure is modest, so that there is no foaming torrent piling its way down the steps, but instead a refreshing trickle of water. Probably it was originally called a *catena d'acqua* [chain of water], rather than a cascade. I assume this is the redirected Garovo stream after which the property was originally named.

At the top of the long green slope is an open temple containing an inevitably giant statue of Hercules, the sort of role model – half-man, half-god routinely completing tasks ordinary men find beyond their comprehension – that sixteenth-century villa owners favoured as the presiding genius on their properties. This statue in fact dates from the eighteenth century, but it is entirely in character. Here,

the visitor is as usual silently invited to guess which one of Hercules's monumental feats is depicted in this statue. This is quite an unusual one. His face contorted with pain and anger, Hercules holds the puny body of Lichas aloft, on the point of throwing him into the sea (or in this case Lake Como, 300 metres/984 feet away) for having tricked him into wearing a poisoned shirt. Behind Hercules is a certain amount of grotto tufa, through which flows the water which feeds the cascades.

ABOVE The hotel occupies a broad frontage along the western shore of Lake Como. Looking south, the promenade at Cernobbio can be seen beyond the shady walk.

OPPOSITE ABOVE The northern boundary of the hotel grounds rises steeply, displaying the romantic crags with their mock fortifications spread out against the rocks and trees.

OPPOSITE BELOW Seasonal bedding in primary colours decorates the lakeside walk under the mature trees. There is always beauty and variety to be viewed on the surface of the lake.

Apart from this extraordinary set piece, a miraculous survival in itself, there is another, later, historic garden laid out along the northern boundary of the hotel grounds. A series of rather precipitous walks is laid out along a steep bank, essentially leading from one folly tower to another. This is supposed to have been created for a retired soldier from the Napoleonic wars to remind him of his military exploits (had he forgotten them?), but this seems a little far-fetched. The folly towers themselves are rugged little structures of several variations on a picturesque theme – some round, some square, with or without mini-battlements, one of them with two storeys – generally built of brick or rubble and roughly rendered to convey an image of instant antiquity. They poke out at various levels along the face of the hill, romantically intermingled with crags and vegetation. Probably the original notion was somewhat in advance of the achieved result. When I was nine I would have loved running from one tower to another, looking out at the epic view. For now, I think glancing up at the scene from the hotel grounds below will do nicely. The real draw here is the nymphaeum and cascade.

RIGHT The view across the parterre, through the richly decorated screen walls and up to the Temple of Hercules, is a miraculous survival of sixteenth-century garden design.

GARDEN LOCATIONS

All the gardens in this book are normally open to the public, but access arrangements vary. The opening times listed here are those in place at the time of writing. Anyone planning a visit would be well advised to check the current situation via the relevant website.

LAKE MAGGIORE

1. ISOLA BELLA
The garden is on the island of the same name in Lake Maggiore, a short distance from the town of Stresa. Boats visit the island from the landing stages at Stresa, Baveno, Pallanza and elsewhere. The garden is open from late March to late October, daily 9 a.m. to 5.30 p.m. The house is also open to visitors: *www.isoleborromee.it/en/home/isola_bella*

2. ISOLA MADRE
The garden is on the island of the same name in Lake Maggiore, a short distance from the town of Pallanza. Boats visit the island from the landing stages at Pallanza, Baveno, Stresa and other towns. The garden is open from late March to late October, daily 9 a.m. to 5.30 p.m. The house is also open to visitors: *www.isoleborromee.it/en/home/isole_madre*

3. VILLA TÁRANTO
Via Vittorio Veneto 111, Verbania-Pallanza
The entrance to the garden is situated on the shore of Lake Maggiore at Pallanza, which is part of Verbania. The garden has its own landing stage on the lake and is open from late March to the end of October, daily 8.30 a.m. to 6.30 p.m.; during October, the garden closes at 4 p.m. The house is not open to visitors: *www.villataranto.it/en*

4. VILLA SAN REMIGIO
Via San Remigio 22, Verbania-Pallanza
At the time of writing, the garden remains closed because of storm damage. It is anticipated that it will reopen in the future. In the past, opening has been on the basis of pre-booked guided visits, organized through the tourist office in Pallanza. The house is not open to visitors: *www.verbania-turismo.it/verbania_town.asp*

5. VILLA DELLA PORTA BOZZOLO
Viale Camillo Bozzolo 5, Casalzuigno, Varese
The garden is in the village of Casalzuigno, in the countryside east of Lake Maggiore. It is well signposted from the main road through the village. The garden, which is owned and run by the Fondo per l'Ambiente Italiano (FAI), is open from March to November, from Wednesday to Sunday, 10 a.m. to 6 p.m.; during October and November, the garden closes at 5 p.m. The house is also open to visitors: *http://eng.fondoambiente.it/beni/villa-della-porta-bozzolo-fai-properties.asp*

6. VILLA CICOGNA MOZZONI
Viale Cicogna 8, Bisúschio, Varese
The garden is on the outskirts of the village of Bisúschio, north of Varese, between Lakes Maggiore and Como. It is well signposted from approaching roads. The villa and garden are open for guided visits on Sundays and public holidays from April to October, 9.30 a.m. to 12 noon, then 2.30 p.m. to 7 p.m. Groups may book in advance on other dates: *www.villacicognamozzoni.it*

7. VILLA PALLAVICINO
Via Sempione Sud, Stresa
The park is a short distance south of Stresa on the main road along the shore of Lake Maggiore. The grounds are open from mid-March to the end of October, daily 9 a.m. to 7 p.m., with the last entry at 5 p.m. The house is not open to the public: *www.parcozoopallavicino.it/index-en.html*

8. ALPINIA
Via Alpinia 22, Alpino di Stresa
The garden is accessible via mountain roads from Stresa on Lake Maggiore, or via the *funivia* [cablecar] from Carciano, on the northern outskirts of Stresa. There is a public boat terminal nearby. The garden is open from mid-April to mid-October, daily 9.30 a.m. to 6 p.m. It is liable to close in adverse weather conditions: *http://en.lagomaggiore.net/24/giardino-alpinia.htm*

9. BOTANIC GARDEN OF THE BRISSAGO ISLANDS
Isole di Brissago, Canton Ticino, Switzerland
The garden is on the larger of the two Brissago islands in the northern, Swiss part of Lake Maggiore. It can be approached by ferry from Brissago or Porto Ronco on the western shore. Passenger boat services on the lake call at Brissago. The garden is open from late March to late October, daily 9 a.m. to 6 p.m. The house is a hotel and restaurant: *www.isolebrissago.ch/en*

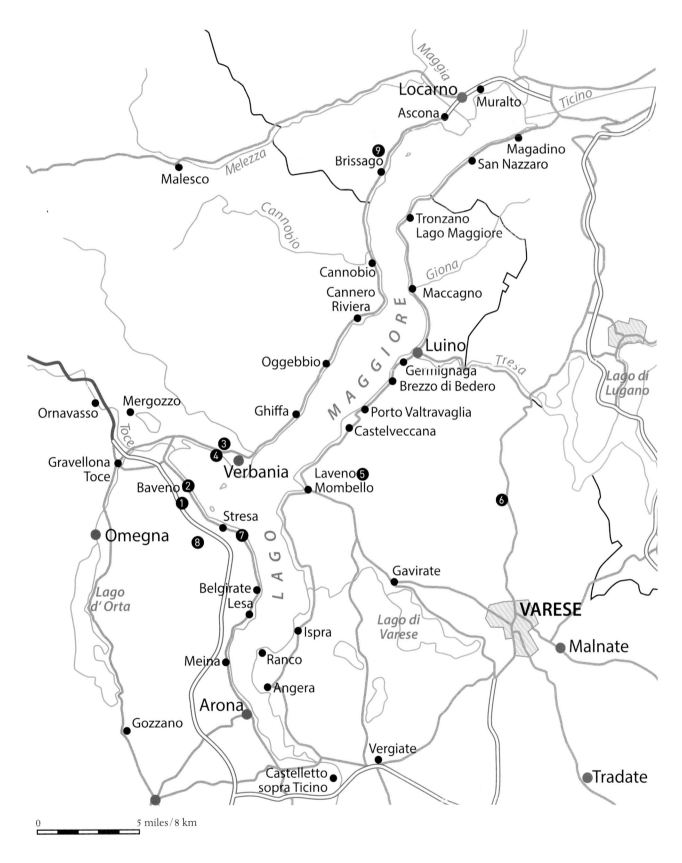

Locarno
Muralto
Ascona
Maggia
Ticino
Malesco
Melezza
Brissago ⑨
Magadino
San Nazzaro
Cannobio
Tronzano
Lago Maggiore
Giona
Cannobio
Cannero
Riviera
Maccagno
Luino
Oggebbio
Germignaga
Brezzo di Bedero
Tresa
Lago di
Lugano
Ornavasso
Mergozzo
Ghiffa
Porto Valtravaglia
Castelveccana
Gravellona
Toce
Toce
Baveno ②
③
④
Verbania
Laveno ⑤
Mombello
M A G G I O R E
Stresa
①
⑦
Omegna
⑧
L A G O
Gavirate
Belgirate
Lesa
Lago
d'Orta
Ispra
Lago di
Varese
VARESE
Meina
Ranco
Malnate
Angera
Arona
Gozzano
Vergiate
Castelletto
sopra Ticino
Tradate

0 5 miles / 8 km

1	ISOLA BELLA	6	VILLA CICOGNA MOZZONI
2	ISOLA MADRE	7	VILLA PALLAVICINO
3	VILLA TÁRANTO	8	ALPINIA
4	VILLA SAN REMIGIO	9	BOTANIC GARDEN OF THE BRISSAGO ISLANDS
5	VILLA DELLA PORTA BOZZOLO		

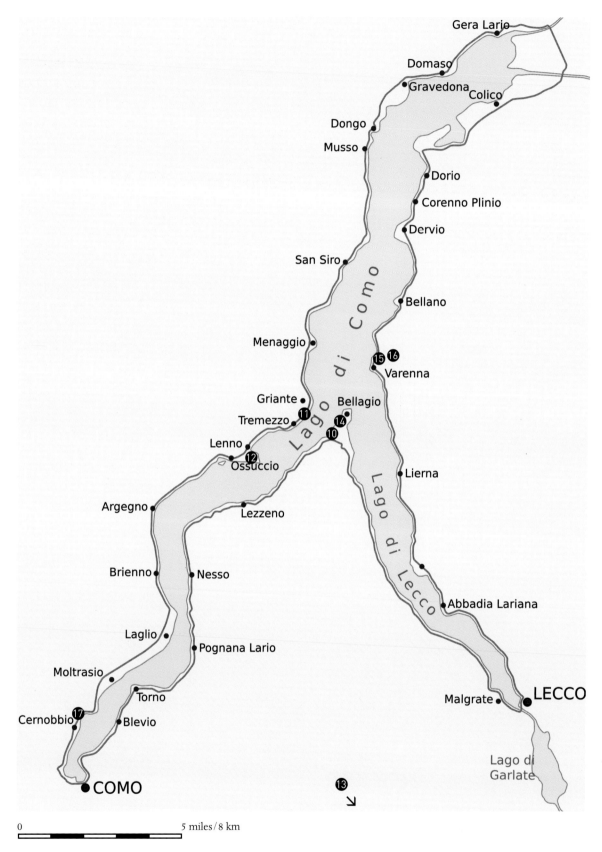

Gera Lario

Domaso

Gravedona

Colico

Dongo

Musso

Dorio

Corenno Plinio

Dervio

San Siro

Bellano

Lago di Como

Menaggio

⑮⑯
Varenna

Griante

Bellagio

Tremezzo
⑪

⑭

Lenno
⑩
⑫
Ossuccio

Lierna

Argegno

Lezzeno

Lago di Lecco

Brienno

Nesso

Abbadia Lariana

Laglio

Pognana Lario

Moltrasio

Malgrate

LECCO

Torno

⑰
Cernobbio

Blevio

Lago di Garlate

COMO

⑬

0   5 miles / 8 km

10 VILLA MELZI
11 VILLA CARLOTTA
12 VILLA DEL BALBIANELLO
13 VILLA SOMMI PICENARDI

14 VILLA SERBELLONI
15 VILLA CIPRESSI
16 VILLA MONASTERO
17 VILLA D'ESTE

LAKE COMO

10. VILLA MELZI

Lungolario Manzoni, Bellagio

The garden is a short walk south of the town centre of Bellagio on Lake Como. It is open from late March to the end of October, daily 9.30 a.m. to 6.30 p.m. The house is not open to the public: *www.giardinidivillamelzi.it*

11. VILLA CARLOTTA

Via Regina 2, Tremezzo, Como

The garden is on the lake shore between Tremezzo and Cadenabbia. It has its own landing stage for the public boat services. The garden is open from early April to mid-October, daily 9 a.m. to 7.30 p.m., but bear in mind that the ticket office closes at 6 p.m. There are openings earlier and later in the season too. The house is also open to visitors: *http://www.villacarlotta.it*

12. VILLA DEL BALBIANELLO

Via Comœdia 5, Tremezzina, Como

The garden lies on a prominent headland in the middle of Lake Como. It is approached from Lenno, the nearest town on the western shore of the lake, which is on the road along the shore, and which also has a landing stage for the public boat service. From there, it is a short walk along the promenade to the Lido, where a regular private boat service takes visitors around the headland to the garden entrance from the lake. It is also possible to walk from Lenno along a signposted route. The garden, which is owned and run by the Fondo per l'Ambiente Italiano (FAI), is open from mid-March to mid-November, daily except Mondays and Wednesdays, 10 a.m. to 6 p.m., with last entry at 5.15 p.m. The house is also open to visitors: *http://eng.fondoambiente.it/beni/villa-del-balbianello-fai-properties.asp*

13. VILLA SOMMI PICENARDI

Via Sommi Picenardi 8, Olgiate Molgora, Lecco

The garden is on the outskirts of the village of Olgiate Molgora, near Lecco on Lake Como. The village has its own railway station on the Lecco–Milan line. The garden is open to visitors by prior arrangement: *www.villasommipicenardi.it/english*

14. VILLA SERBELLONI

Piazza della Chiesa 14, Bellagio

The garden belongs to the Rockefeller Foundation, and is opened regularly for tours led by guides from the tourist authority in Bellagio. These tours take place from mid-March to the end of October, daily except Mondays, at 11 a.m. and 2.30 p.m. The booking office and point of departure are in the medieval tower in the Piazza della Chiesa, near the church of San Giacomo, in Bellagio. The garden should not be confused with the nearby Grand Hotel Villa Serbelloni, which is a separate establishment. The house is not open to the public: *www.bellagiolakecomo.com/bellagio-lake-como-italy/POI-points-of-interest/villa-serbelloni-garden*

15. VILLA CIPRESSI

Via IV Novembre 18, Varenna

The garden is part of the Hotel Villa Cipressi in Varenna, which is on the eastern shore road along Lake Como. Varenna has a railway station and a public boat landing stage. The hotel staff admit visitors to the garden only by ticket from reception: *www.hotelvillacipressi.it/en/index.html*

16. VILLA MONASTERO

Via G. Polvani 4, Varenna

Despite the address, the entrance to the Villa Monastero is next door to the Villa Cipressi. The property is owned by the local authority. The garden is open from March to the end of October, daily 9.30 a.m. to 5 p.m. The house is also open to visitors: *www.villamonastero.eu/index.php/en*

17. VILLA D'ESTE

Via Regina 40, Cernobbio

The garden is part of the grounds of the Hotel Villa D'Este at Cernobbio, on the western shore of Lake Como. It may be visited by arrangement with the hotel management: *www.villadeste.com/en/13/home.aspx*

INDEX

ACKNOWLEDGMENTS
FROM STEVEN DESMOND AND MARIANNE MAJERUS

Many people have helped in different ways over the years to provide us with the opportunity to write this book. They include the owners, management and staff of all the gardens described. Among those who have been especially kind, helpful, informative, patient, understanding or otherwise inspirational we wish to thank the following: Serena Bertolucci, Joanna Chisholm, Eleonore and Jacopo Cicogna Mozzoni, Neill Coleman, Jane Crawley, Gabriella De Paoli, Amanda Desmond, Michela Gatti, Gianfranco Giustina, Susan Gullen, Helen Griffin, Federica Long, Monica Mandelli, Brian Manning, Giovanni Battista Margaroli, Arianna Osti, Carmen Pedretti, Martin Randall, Arianna Sancassani, Serena Sogno, Azzurra Sommi Picenardi, Daniela Vaninetti, the management of the Hotel Villa D'Este and the staff of the Grand Hotel Villa Serbelloni.

PICTURE CREDITS

All images are copyright of Marianne Majerus except for the following:
Alamy: 108 © Giovanni Tagini; 110 © Federico Rano.
author: 100 (bottom), 104, 105, 111, 112, 114, 115, 116, 117, 127, 177 (bottom), 190, 192, 193 (bottom), 197, 202, 203.
author's archive collection: 8, 9, 18, 26, 40, 41 (top), 70, 72 (bottom), 84 (top), 135 (top), 207.
Fondo per l'Ambiente Italiano: 165 (top).
Fotolia: 215 © Rainer Lesniewski.
Museo del Paesaggio, Verbania-Pallanza: 78 (bottom), 79 (top).
Museo Villa Carlotta: 144 (bottom).
Shutterstock: 102 © Raffaella Calzoni; 106–7 © Claudiovidri; 193 (top), 194–5, 198, 200 © Alexander Chaikin; 196 © Malgorzata Kistryn; 201 © Capricorn Studio; 214 © Rainer Lesniewski.

FURTHER READING

Anon [Gladys Huntington], *Madame Solario*, London: Heinemann, 1956

Bagot, Richard and Ragg, Laura M., *The Italian Lakes*, London: A. & C. Black, 1905

Burnet, Gilbert, *Some Letters Containing an Account of What Seemed Most Remarkable in Switzerland, Italy, &c.*, Rotterdam: Abraham Acher, 1686

Laing, Samuel, *Notes of a Traveller on the Social and Political State of France, Prussia, Switzerland, Italy, and other Parts of Europe, during the Present Century*, London: Longman, Brown, Green & Longmans, 1842

Le Blond, Mrs Aubrey, *The Old Gardens of Italy: How to Visit Them*, London: John Lane, Bodley Head, 1912

McEacharn, Neil, *The Villa Táranto, A Scotsman's Garden in Italy*, London: Country Life, 1954

Masson, Georgina, *Italian Gardens*, London: Thames & Hudson, 1961

Masson, Georgina, *Italian Villas and Palaces*, London: Thames & Hudson, 1959

O'Conor, Matthew, *Picturesque and Historical Recollections During a Tour through Belgium, Germany, France and Switzerland in the Summer Vacation of 1835*, London: Wm S. Orr, 1837

Pisoni, Carlo Alessandro, Parachini, Leonardo, Monferrini, Sergio and Invernizzi, Dante, *Amor di Pianta: Giardinieri, Floricoltori, Vivaisti sul Verbano 1750–1950*, Verbania: La Compagnia de' Bindoni et alia, 2005 copy SCD

Selvafolta, Ornella and Cottini, Paolo, *I Giardini di Villa Melzi d'Eril a Bellagio*, Milan: Villa Melzi/Cisalpino, 2012

Stendhal, *Diario del Viaggio in Brianza*, 1818; modern edition BellaviteSelvafolta, Ornella and Cottini, Paolo, *I Giardini di Villa Melzi d'Eril a Bellagio*, Milan: Villa Melzi/Cisalpino, 2009

Stendhal, *Rome, Naples and Florence*, Paris: Edouard Champion, 1919

Taine, Hippolyte, *Voyage en Italie 1866*, translated as *Italy: Florence and Venice*, trans J. Durand, 4th edn New York: Holt & Williams, 1873

Twain, Mark, *The Innocents Abroad*, Hartford: American Publishing Company, 1869

Wharton, Edith: *Italian Villas and their Gardens*, New York: Century, 1904

HALF TITLE An upper terrace on Isola Bella.

TITLE PAGE The garden glimpsed through the loggia at the Villa Cicogna Mozzoni.

CONTENTS PAGE A white peacock on a rail, Isola Bella.